MENSA

MIGHTY MIND BENDERS

WORD PUZZLES

M R

E E   A

S   I D

K

D

II

E

R

U

S

D E   A R E A

E

I D   E E

MENSA

MIGHTY MIND BENDERS

WORD PUZZLES

HAROLD GALE

STANLEY PAUL
London

CARLTON
Books

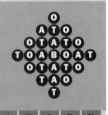

First published 1993

1 3 5 7 9 10 8 6 4 2

Text © Mensa Publications Limited 1993
Design © Carlton Books Limited 1993

Mensa Publications have asserted their right under the Copyright, Designs and Patents Act, 1988 to be identified as the author of this work

First published in the United Kingdom in 1993 by
Stanley Paul and Company Ltd
Random House, 20 Vauxhall Bridge Road, London SW1V 2SA

Random House Australia (Pty) Limited
20 Alfred Street, Milsons Point, Sydney,
New South Wales 2061, Australia

Random House New Zealand Limited
18 Poland Road, Glenfield,
Auckland 10, New Zealand

Random House South Africa (Pty) Limited
PO Box 337, Bergvlei, South Africa

Random House UK Limited Reg. No. 954009

A CIP catalogue record for this book
is available from the British Library

ISBN 0-09-178038-1

Designed by Jacqui Ellis

Printed in Spain

INTRODUCTION

PUZZLES which involve the use of the English language are notoriously difficult to produce. Unfortunately the differences between the English used in Europe and the English used elsewhere are considerable. This book uses words which, hopefully, match the use of English throughout the world. The main dictionaries used are *Webster's New World Dictionary* and the *Collins English Dictionary*.

Word puzzles are fun. This has been proved over and over again in the many puzzle features which have been printed in major newspapers and magazines throughout the world. At the time of writing the British Rail first-class passenger magazine, *Intercity*, prints a page of similar puzzles each issue. The British newspaper, *Today*, carries a puzzle per day and this is in the process of world-wide syndication. Many in-flight magazines from the far-east to the Caribbean use similar puzzles. My problem is that I have to devise them. Fortunately I have an extremely able helper in Carolyn Skitt. She checks, criticizes and improves on many of the puzzles produced. Without Carolyn this book would still be in the making. Help has also come from other quarters. Joanne Harris spent a great deal of time perfecting the tinted puzzles, Bobby Raikhy worked on the many diagrammatic styles, and David Ballheimer checked the proofs. But what of Mensa?

If you can solve the puzzles can you join the organization? You should have no problem. These are fun puzzles but they are by no means easy. If you can work these out, the Mensa test should prove to be no hurdle and you should easily qualify. Once you have joined you will find a feeling of self-satisfaction that very few experience in a life-time. You will meet people of different walks of life but of similar brain power. A scientist can meet a poet; a composer, an architect. The broadening of the intellectual vision is amazing. The new horizon is formidable, but challenging. I invite you to join this ever-expanding group of people, where race, religion or political persuasion are not blocks but keys: keys to opening new doors of understanding, friendship and considered discussion.

There are 40,000 Mensa members in the British Isles alone. There are over 50,000 in the USA. There are 120,000 throughout the world. Write to: Mensa (MWP), Mensa House, St John's Square, Wolverhampton WV2 1AH. We will send you details and a home-screening IQ test.

HAROLD GALE
Executive Director of British Mensa
March, 1993.

Take 10 minutes only to complete the test.

1 If a circle is one how many is an octagon?

2 There are 1,200 elephants in a herd. Some have pink and blue stripes, some are all pink and some are all blue. Of these one third are pure pink. Is it true that 400 elephants are definitely blue?

3 Which vowel comes midway between J and T?

4 Which number comes next in this series of numbers?

1 2 3 5 7 11 13 ?

5 Which letter comes next in this series of letters?

B A C B D C E D F ?

6 Which of these is the odd one out?

CAT DOG HAMSTER RABBIT ELK

7 Which word can be added to the end of GRASS and the beginning of SCAPE to form two other English words?

8 The zoo has two lions. A lion eats three pounds of meat each day. A lioness eats two pounds of meat each day and a lion cub eats one pound of meat. The delivery for today is two pounds of meat and that is all the meat available for the zoo. Must any or both of the lions go hungry?

9 If six minus one is worth nine and seven minus five is worth one. How much is six plus ten worth?

10 Which word of four letters can be added to the front of the following words to create other English words?

CARD BOX CODE BAG HASTE

Answers

1	8.
2	No.
3	O.
4	17. (They are all prime numbers.)
5	E.
6	Elk.
7	Land.
8	No, they could be lion cubs.
9	9. Value of Roman numerals in words, if any, either subtracted or added.
10	Post.

Score	Comment	Possible IQ
10	Excellent	160
9	Very Good Indeed	155
8	Mensa Level	148
7	Good	130
6	Above Average	115
5	Average	100
4	Below Average	90
3	Well Below Average	80
2	Poor	65
1	Very Poor Indeed	50

Now try this one:
Your watch was correct at midnight but then began to gain two and a half minutes every hour. It stopped two hours ago showing quarter past six in the morning. What should the watch be showing?

If you think you have the correct answer send it to Mensa on a postcard or the back of an envelope and you will receive a certificate of merit, along with Mensa details. The address to reply to is:
Mensa House, St John's Square, Wolverhampton WV2 1AH.

WORD PUZZLE 1

Place one letter in the middle of this diagram. Four five-letter
words can now be rearranged from each straight line of letters.
What is the letter and what are the words?

ANSWER 62

WORD PUZZLE 2

Arrange the tiles in this diagram so that they form a square.
When this is done correctly four words can be read down and
across. What are the words?

ANSWER 10

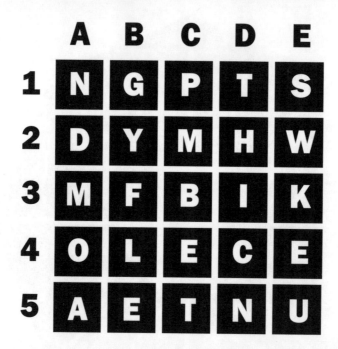

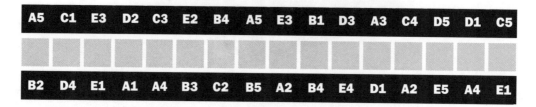

WORD PUZZLE 3

Select one of the two letters from the grid, in accordance with the reference shown, and place it in the word frame. When the correct letters have been chosen a sixteen-letter word can be read.
What is the word?

ANSWER 103

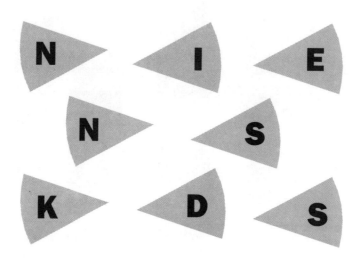

WORD PUZZLE 4

Make a circle out of these shapes.
When the correct circle has been found an English word can be read clockwise. What is the word?

ANSWER 51

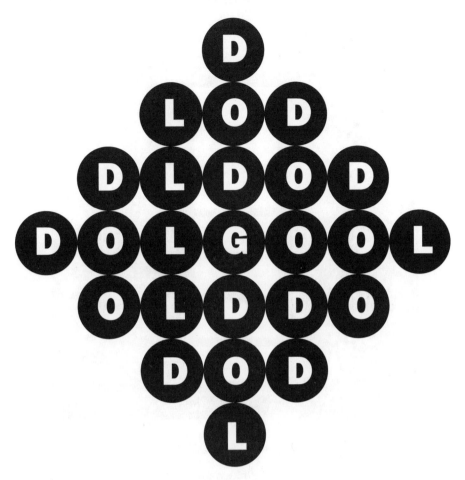

WORD PUZZLE 5

Move from circle to touching circle collecting the letters of GOLD.
Always start at the G.
How many different ways are there to do this?

ANSWER 92

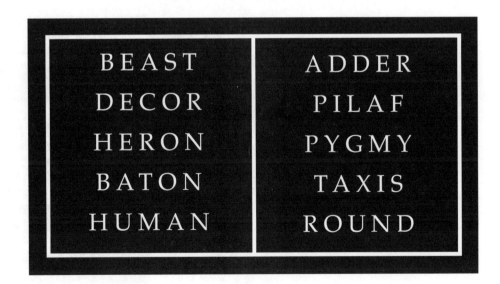

WORD PUZZLE 6

Six of the words in the diagram are associated for some
reason. Find the words and then work out whether SHELL belongs
to the group.

ANSWER 40

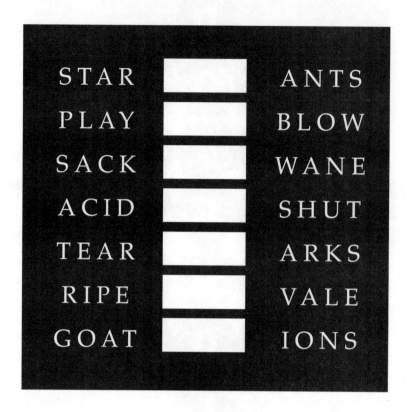

STAR		ANTS
PLAY		BLOW
SACK		WANE
ACID		SHUT
TEAR		ARKS
RIPE		VALE
GOAT		IONS

WORD PUZZLE 7

Change the second letter of each word to the left and the right.
Two other English words must be formed. Place the letter used in
the empty section. When this has been completed for all the words
another English word can be read down. What is the word?

ANSWER 82

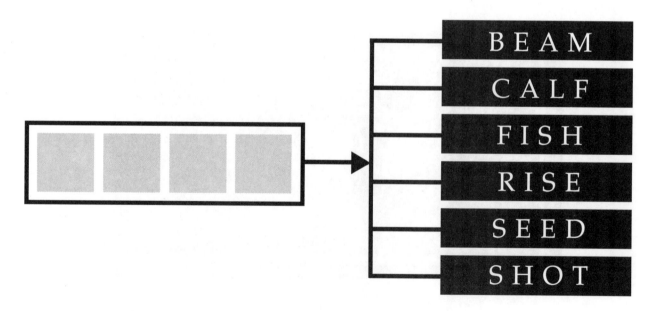

WORD PUZZLE 8

Which English word of four letters can be attached to the front of
the words shown in the diagram to create six other words?

ANSWER 30

WORD PUZZLE 9

Complete the word ladder by changing one letter of each word
per step. The newly created word must be found in the dictionary.
What are the words to turn SEEDS to GRASS?

ANSWER 72

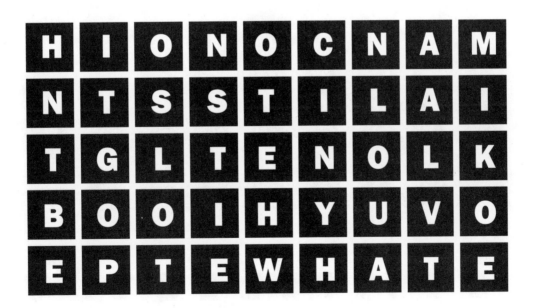

WORD PUZZLE 10

A quotation has been written in this diagram. Find the start letter
and move from square to touching square until you have found it.
What is the quotation and to whom is it attributed?

ANSWER 20

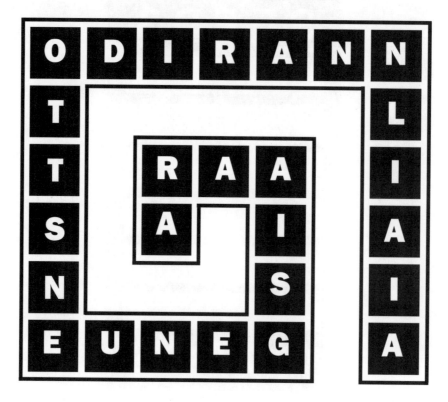

WORD PUZZLE 11

The names of three countries are to be found in the diagram.
The letters of the names are in the order they normally appear.
What are the countries?

ANSWER 61

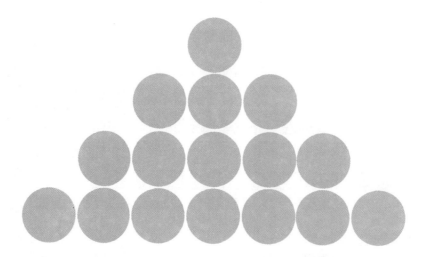

A A D D I I I L L L Q T U V W Y

WORD PUZZLE 12

Place the letters shown into the diagram in such a way
that three words can be read across and one down the middle.
What are the words?

ANSWER 9

WORD PUZZLE 13

Start at the bottom letter M and move from circle to touching circle to the N at the top right. How many different ways are there of collecting the nine letters of MANHATTAN?

ANSWER 102

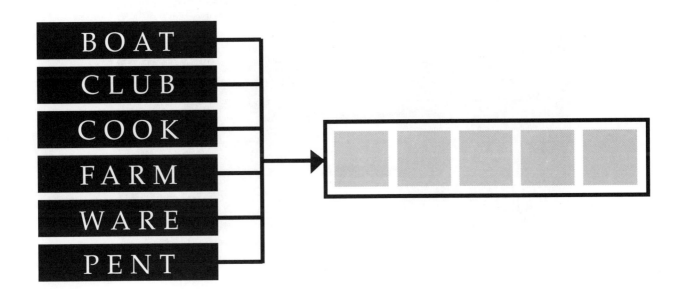

WORD PUZZLE 14

Which English word of five letters can be attached to the back of the words shown in the diagram to create six other words?

ANSWER 50

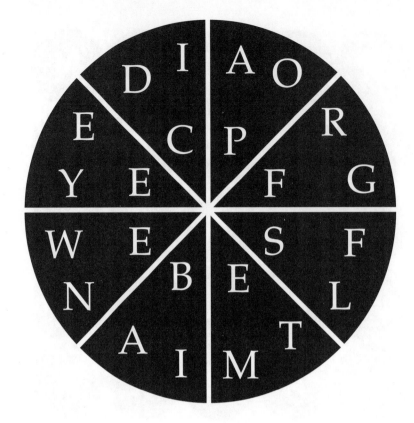

WORD PUZZLE 15

Select one letter from each of the segments.
When the correct letters have been found a word of eight letters
can be read clockwise. What is the word?

ANSWER 91

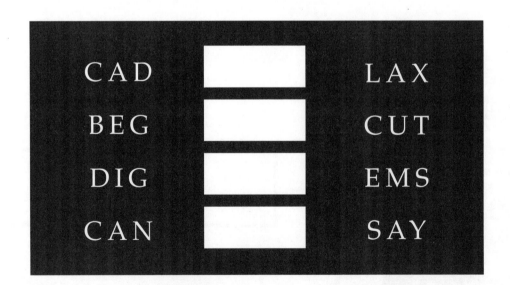

WORD PUZZLE 16

Place two letters in the empty space which, when added to the
end of the words to the left and to the beginning of the right, form
other English words. When this is completed another word
can be read downwards. What is the word?

ANSWER 39

N O F S

Q O E E

C A R Y

M U T S

WORD PUZZLE 17

Take the letters and arrange
them correctly in the column
under which they appear.
Once this has been done an
historical character will appear.
Who is the person?

ANSWER 81

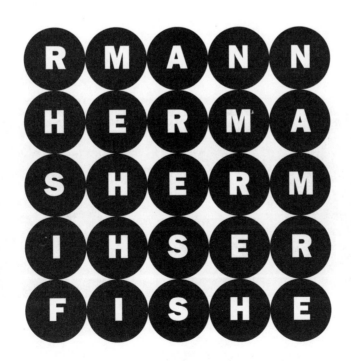

WORD PUZZLE 18

Start at the bottom letter F and move from circle to touching circle
to the N at the top right. How many different ways are there of
collecting the nine letters of FISHERMAN?

ANSWER 29

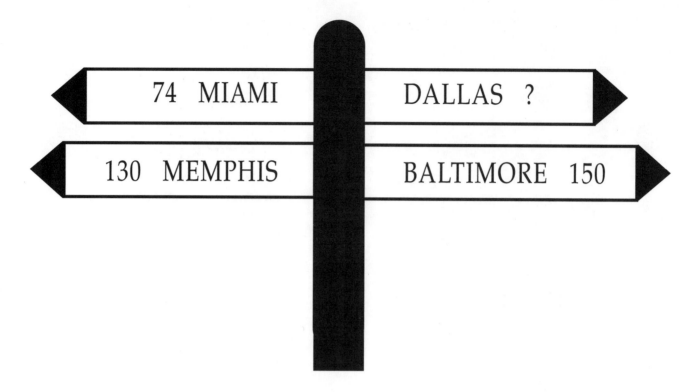

WORD PUZZLE 19

This is a meaningless signpost but there is a twisted form of
logic behind the figures. Discover the logic and find the distance to
Dallas. How far is it?

ANSWER 71

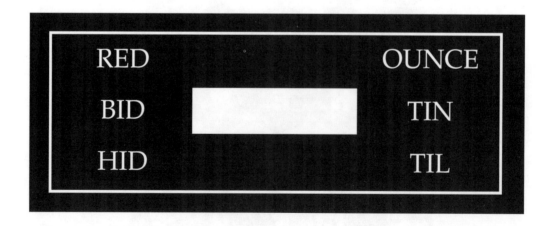

WORD PUZZLE 20

Place an English word of THREE letters in the empty space. This
word, when added to the end of the three words to the left and to
the beginning of the three words to the right, will form six other
words. What is the word?

ANSWER 19

WORD PUZZLE 21

Arrange the tiles in this diagram so that they form a square.
When this is done correctly four words can be read down and
across. What are the words?

ANSWER 8

WORD PUZZLE 22

Place one letter in the middle of this diagram. Four five-letter
words can now be rearranged from each straight line of letters.
What is the letter and what are the words?

ANSWER 60

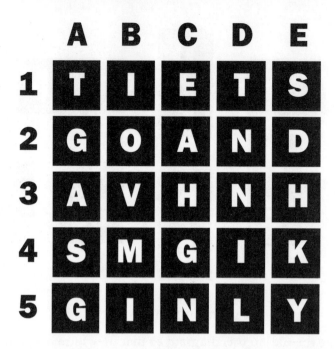

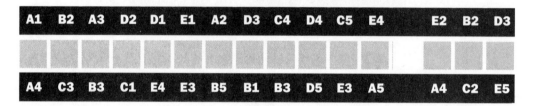

WORD PUZZLE 23

Select one of the two letters from the grid, in accordance with the
reference shown, and place it in the word frame. When the correct
letters have been chosen an occasion can be read.
What is the occasion?

ANSWER 101

WORD PUZZLE 24

Make a circle out of these shapes.
When the correct circle has been found an English word can be
read clockwise. What is the word?

ANSWER 49

BURNT	EVENT
COUNT	CADET
MERIT	FAULT
FLINT	CARAT
ABBOT	GIANT

WORD PUZZLE 25

Five of the words in the diagram are associated for some reason. Find the words and then work out whether PLANT belongs to the group.

ANSWER 90

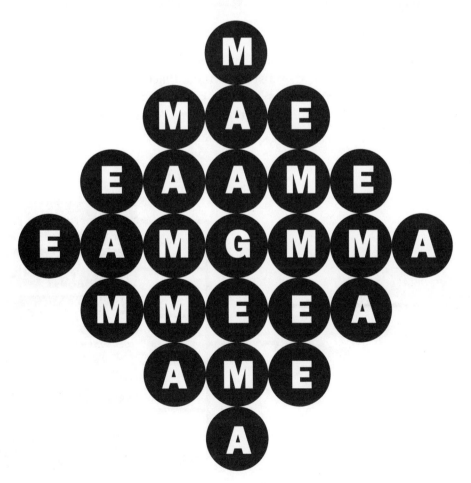

WORD PUZZLE 26

Move from circle to touching circle collecting the letters of GAME.
Always start at the G.
How many different ways are there to do this?

ANSWER 38

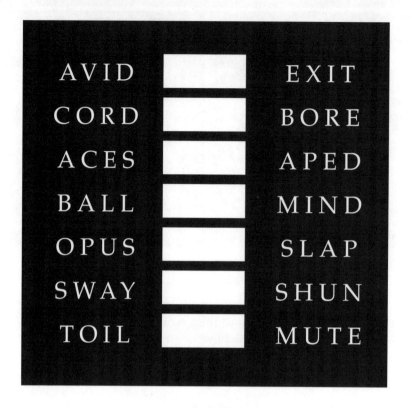

WORD PUZZLE 27

Change the second letter of each word to the left and the right.
Two other English words must be formed. Place the letter used in
the empty section. When this has been completed for all the words
another English word can be read down. What is the word?

ANSWER 80

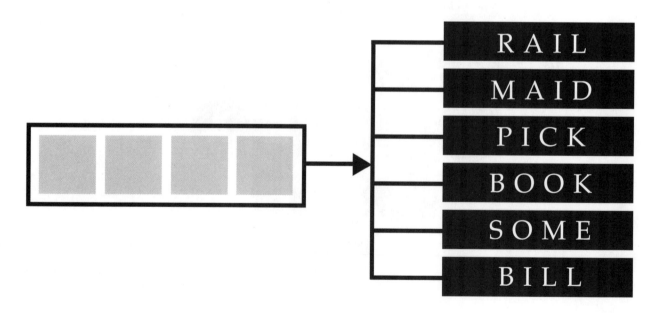

WORD PUZZLE 28

Which English word of four letters can be attached to the front of
the words shown in the diagram to create six other words?

ANSWER 28

WORD PUZZLE 29

Complete the word ladder by changing one letter of each word
per step. The newly created word must be found in the dictionary.
What are the words to turn CHOP to TREE?

ANSWER 70

WORD PUZZLE 30

A quotation has been written in this diagram. Find the start letter
and move from square to touching square until you have found it.
What is the quotation and to whom is it attributed?

ANSWER 18

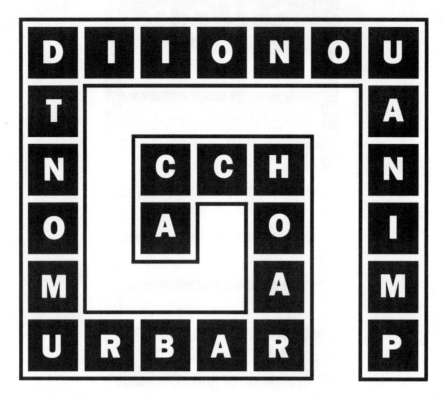

WORD PUZZLE 31

The names of four musical instruments are to be found in the
diagram. The letters of the names are in the order they normally
appear. What are the musical instruments?

ANSWER 59

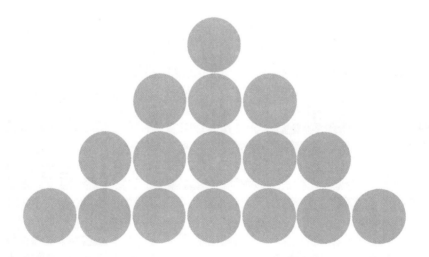

AEFFFFIIIMRRRRST

WORD PUZZLE 32

Place the letters shown into the diagram in such a way
that three words can be read across and one down the middle.
What are the words?

ANSWER 7

WORD PUZZLE 33

Start at the bottom letter N and move from circle to touching circle
to the E at the top right. How many different ways are there of
collecting the nine letters of NECTARINE?

ANSWER 100

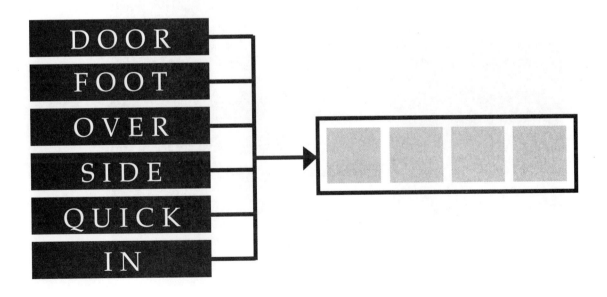

WORD PUZZLE 34

Which English word of four letters can be attached to the back of
the words shown in the diagram to create six other words?

ANSWER 48

WORD PUZZLE 35

Select one letter from each of the segments.
When the correct letters have been found a word of eight letters
can be read clockwise. What is the word?

ANSWER 89

WORD PUZZLE 36

Place two letters in the empty space which, when added to the
end of the words to the left and to the beginning of the right, form
other English words. When this is completed another word
can be read down. What is the word?

ANSWER 37

R E R N

T S A S

O E I M

M H C A

WORD PUZZLE 37

Take the letters and arrange them correctly in the column under which they appear. Once this has been done a famous person will appear. Who is the person?

ANSWER 79

AFTER THE DOUBLE WEDDING, THE TWO • • • • • • WALKED THROUGH THE HALL, WHICH WAS LITTERED WITH THE • • • • • • FROM THE PARTY HELD THE PREVIOUS NIGHT.

WORD PUZZLE 38

Two words using the same letters in their construction can be used to replace the dots in this sentence. The sentence will then make sense. Each dot is one letter. What are the words?

ANSWER 27

APPLES	69
PEARS	59
PEACHES	?
MELONS	78

WORD PUZZLE 39

Here are some fruit.
The number of each is set alongside the
name of the fruit in the diagram.
There is a relationship between the number
and the letters of the names.
How many peaches are there?

ANSWER 69

LADY		WISE
APE		ABLE
GOD		NESS

WORD PUZZLE 40

Place an English word of FOUR letters in the empty space. This
word, when added to the end of the three words to the left and to
the beginning of the three words to the right, will form six other
words. What is the word?

ANSWER 17

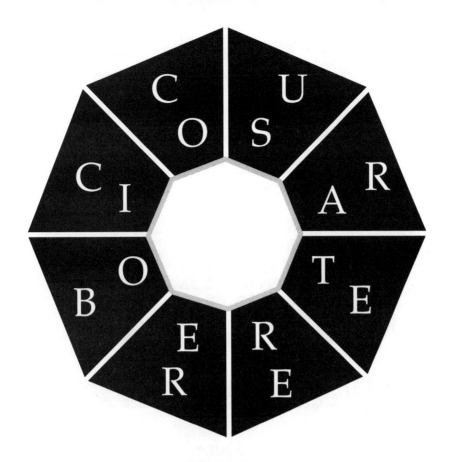

WORD PUZZLE 41

Place one letter in the middle of this diagram. Four five-letter words can now be rearranged from each straight line of letters. What is the letter and what are the words?

ANSWER 58

WORD PUZZLE 42

Arrange the tiles in this diagram so that they form a square. When this is done correctly four words can be read downwards and across. What are the words?

ANSWER 6

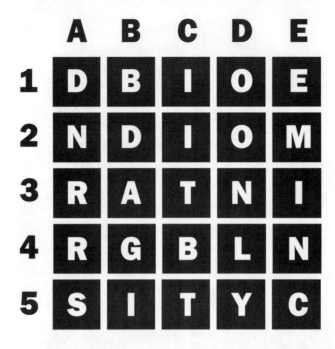

	A	B	C	D	E
1	D	B	I	O	E
2	N	D	I	O	M
3	R	A	T	N	I
4	R	G	B	L	N
5	S	I	T	Y	C

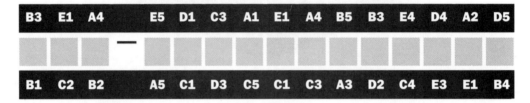

B3	E1	A4		E5	D1	C3	A1	E1	A4	B5	B3	E4	D4	A2	D5
			—												
B1	C2	B2		A5	C1	D3	C5	C1	C3	A3	D2	C4	E3	E1	B4

WORD PUZZLE 43

Select one of the two letters from the grid, in accordance with the reference shown, and place it in the word frame. When the correct letters have been chosen a word can be read.
What is the word?

ANSWER 99

WORD PUZZLE 44

Make a circle out of these shapes.
When the correct circle has been found an English word can be read clockwise. What is the word?

ANSWER 47

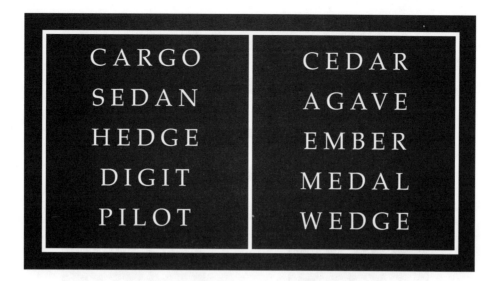

CARGO	CEDAR
SEDAN	AGAVE
HEDGE	EMBER
DIGIT	MEDAL
PILOT	WEDGE

WORD PUZZLE 45

Five of the words in the diagram are associated for some
reason. Find the words and then work out whether SYRUP belongs
to the group.

ANSWER 88

WORD PUZZLE 46

Move from circle to touching circle collecting the letters of FROG.
Always start at the F.
How many different ways are there to do this?

ANSWER 36

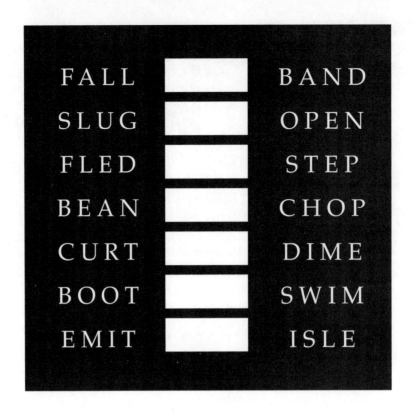

FALL   BAND

SLUG   OPEN

FLED   STEP

BEAN   CHOP

CURT   DIME

BOOT   SWIM

EMIT   ISLE

WORD PUZZLE 47

Change the second letter of each word to the left and the right.
Two other English words must be formed. Place the letter used in
the empty section. When this has been completed for all the words
another English word can be read down. What is the word?

ANSWER 78

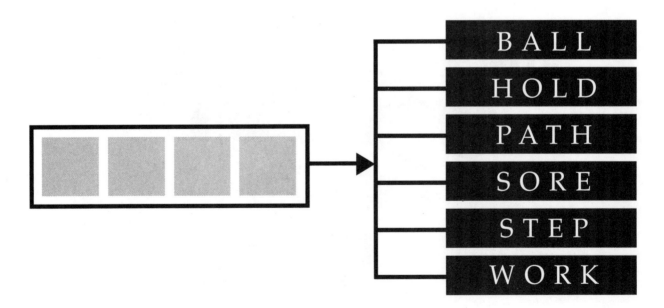

BALL

HOLD

PATH

SORE

STEP

WORK

WORD PUZZLE 48

Which English word of four letters can be attached to the front of
the words shown in the diagram to create six other words?

ANSWER 26

WORD PUZZLE 49

Complete the word ladder by changing
one letter of each word per step.
The newly created word must be found
in the dictionary.
What are the words to turn
RIVER to BANKS?

ANSWER 68

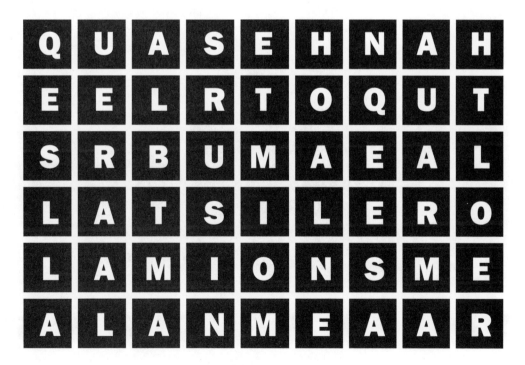

WORD PUZZLE 50

A quotation has been written in this diagram. Find the start letter
and move from square to touching square until you have found it.
What is the quotation and to whom is it attributed?

ANSWER 16

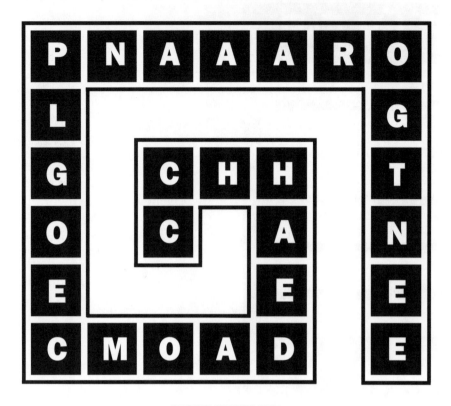

WORD PUZZLE 51

The names of three drinks are to be found in the diagram.
The letters of the names are in the order they normally appear.
What are the drinks?

ANSWER 57

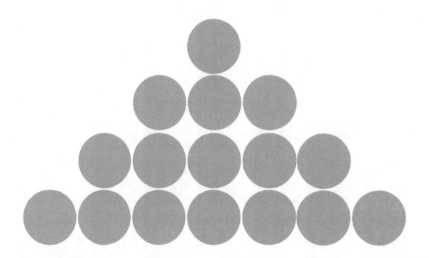

ABCEEEEEGIMORSVY

WORD PUZZLE 52

Place the letters shown into the diagram in such a way
that three words can be read across and one down the middle.
What are the words?

ANSWER 5

WORD PUZZLE 53

Start at the letter L and move from circle to touching circle to the H
at the top right. How many different ways are there of collecting
the nine letters of LABYRINTH?

ANSWER 98

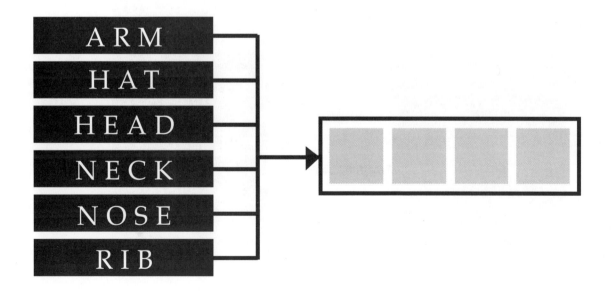

WORD PUZZLE 54

Which English word of four letters can be attached to the back of
the words shown in the diagram to create six other words?

ANSWER 46

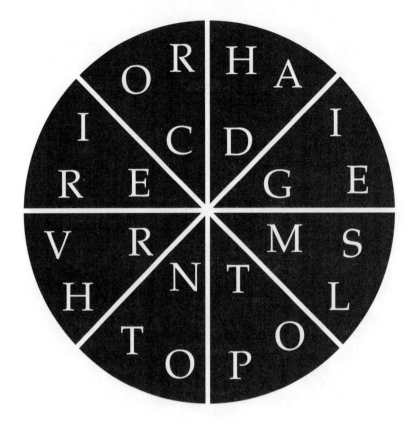

WORD PUZZLE 55

Select one letter from each of the segments.
When the correct letters have been found a word of eight letters
can be read clockwise. What is the word?

ANSWER 87

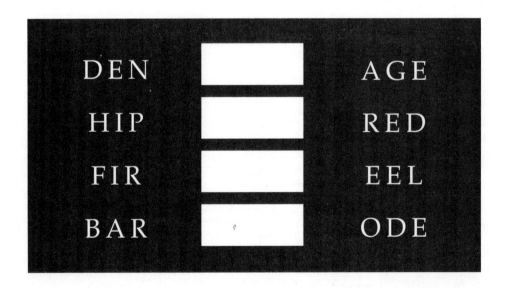

DEN ☐ AGE

HIP ☐ RED

FIR ☐ EEL

BAR ☐ ODE

WORD PUZZLE 56

Place two letters in the empty space which, when added to the
end of the words to the left and to the beginning of the right, form
other English words. When this is completed another word
can be read downwards. What is the word?

ANSWER 35

P H M V

O Y O E

T L W S

E D E H

WORD PUZZLE 57

Take the letters and arrange
them correctly in the column
under which they appear.
Once this has been done a movie
title will appear.
What is the movie?

ANSWER 77

AUSTRALIA	960
MADAGASCAR	1152
IRELAND	576
CUBA	?

WORD PUZZLE 58

The distances on this departure board are fictitious. They bear a
relationship to the letters in the names, What should replace the
question mark ?

ANSWER 25

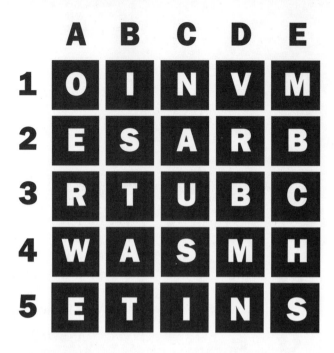

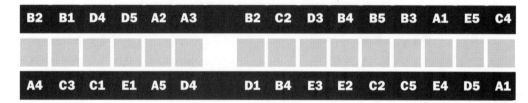

WORD PUZZLE 59

Select one of the two letters from the grid, in accordance with the reference shown, and place it in the word frame. When the correct letters have been chosen two linked words can be read.
What are the words?

ANSWER 67

WORD PUZZLE 60

Place an English word of FOUR letters in the empty space. This word, when added to the end of the three words to the left and to the beginning of the three words to the right, will form six other words. What is the word?

ANSWER 15

WORD PUZZLE 61

Place one letter in the middle of this diagram. Four five-letter
words can now be rearranged from each straight line of letters.
What is the letter and what are the words?

ANSWER 56

WORD PUZZLE 62

Arrange the tiles in this diagram so that they form a square.
When this is done correctly four words can be read down and
across. What are the words?

ANSWER 4

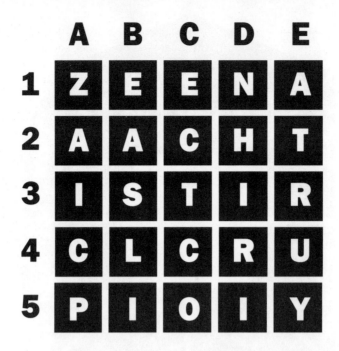

	A	B	C	D	E
1	Z	E	E	N	A
2	A	A	C	H	T
3	I	S	T	I	R
4	C	L	C	R	U
5	P	I	O	I	Y

A4	C1	D1	C5	B2	D2	C5	B1	D4	C5	A1	B5	C3	B3	C5	E5
A1	D2	E1	E3	A5	C2	C3	B3	A3	D5	B3	A2	E2	B5	C4	D1

WORD PUZZLE 63

Select one of the two letters from the grid, in accordance with the reference shown, and place it in the word frame. When the correct letters have been chosen a sixteen-letter word can be read.
What is the word?

ANSWER 97

WORD PUZZLE 64

Make a circle out of these shapes.
When the correct circle has been found an English word can be read clockwise. What is the word?

ANSWER 45

COYPU	MAYOR
AROMA	BISON
NYMPH	NIGHT
IDYLL	RABBI
BUYER	ABYSS

WORD PUZZLE 65

Five of the words in the diagram are associated for some
reason. Find the words and then work out whether STYLE belongs
to the group.

ANSWER 86

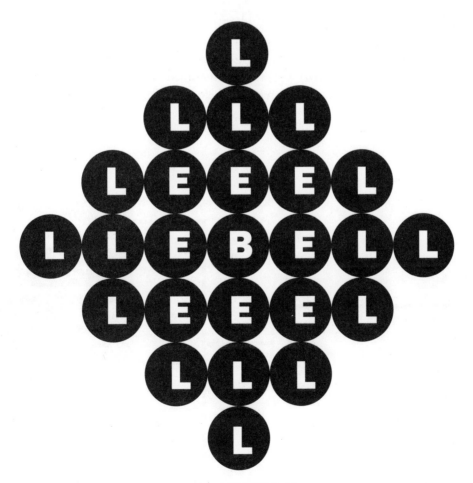

WORD PUZZLE 66

Move from circle to touching circle collecting the letters of BELL.
Always start at the B.
How many different ways are there to do this?

ANSWER 34

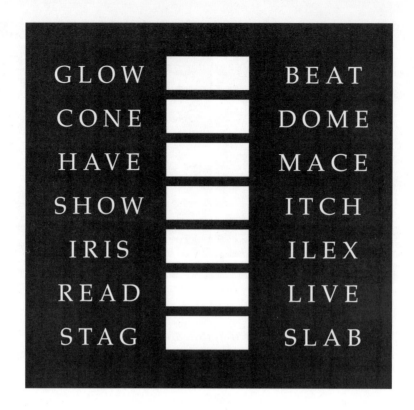

WORD PUZZLE 67

Change the second letter of each word to the left and the right.
Two other English words must be formed. Place the letter used in
the empty section. When this has been completed for all the words
another English word can be read down. What is the word?

ANSWER 76

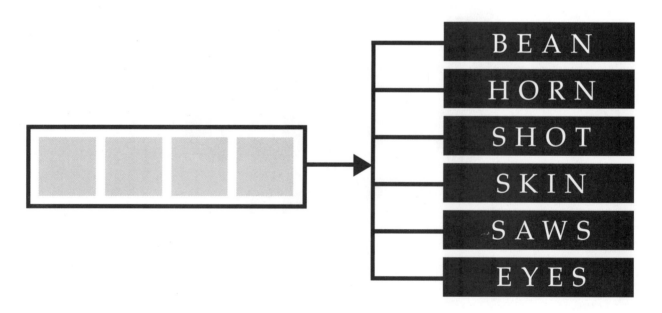

WORD PUZZLE 68

Which English word of four letters can be attached to the front of
the words shown in the diagram to create six other words?

ANSWER 24

PONY

CART

WORD PUZZLE 69

Complete the word ladder by changing one letter of each word
per step. The newly created word must be found in the dictionary.
What are the words to turn PONY to CART?

ANSWER 66

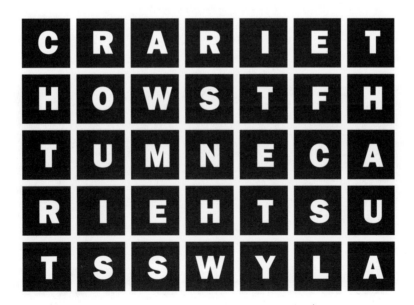

C	R	A	R	I	E	T
H	O	W	S	T	F	H
T	U	M	N	E	C	A
R	I	E	H	T	S	U
T	S	S	W	Y	L	A

WORD PUZZLE 70

A quotation has been written in this diagram. Find the start letter
and move from square to touching square until you have found it.
What is the quotation and to whom is it attributed?

ANSWER 14

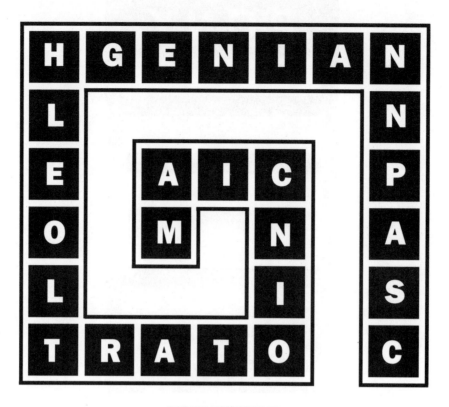

WORD PUZZLE 71

The names of three foods are to be found in the diagram.
The letters of the names are in the order they normally appear.
What are the foods?

ANSWER 55

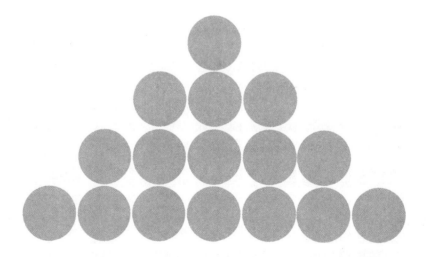

A B D E E E J K L L M N O T W W

WORD PUZZLE 72

Place the letters shown into the diagram in such a way
that three words can be read across and one down the middle.
What are the words?

ANSWER 3

WORD PUZZLE 73

Start at the letter B and move from circle to touching circle to the A
at the top right. How many different ways are there of collecting
the nine letters of BALLERINA?

ANSWER 96

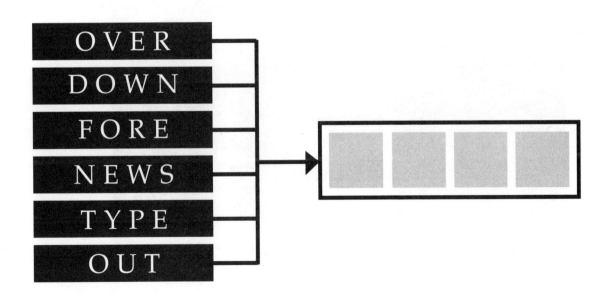

WORD PUZZLE 74

Which English word of four letters can be attached to the back of
the words shown in the diagram to create six other words?

ANSWER 44

WORD PUZZLE 75

Select one letter from each of the segments.
When the correct letters have been found a word of eight letters
can be read clockwise. What is the word?

ANSWER 85

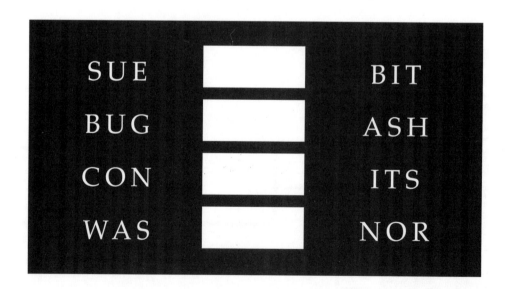

WORD PUZZLE 76

Place two letters in the empty space which, when added to the
end of the words to the left and to the beginning of the right, form
other English words. When this is completed another word
can be read down. What is the word?

ANSWER 33

T A W S
E V E I
L S N O
D H W C

WORD PUZZLE 77

Take the letters and arrange them correctly in the column under which they appear. Once this has been done a movie title will appear. What is the movie?

ANSWER 75

16 NEWARK   CHICAGO ?

20 PORTLAND   CHARLESTON 26

WORD PUZZLE 78

This is a meaningless signpost but there is a twisted form of logic behind the figures. Discover the logic and find the distance to Chicago. How far is it?

ANSWER 65

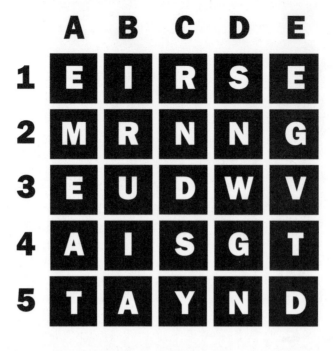

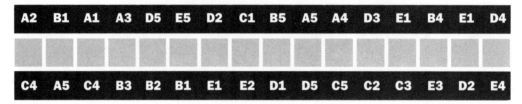

WORD PUZZLE 79

Select one of the two letters from the grid, in accordance with the
reference shown, and place it in the word frame. When the correct
letters have been chosen a sixteen-letter word can be read.
What is the word?

ANSWER 23

WORD PUZZLE 80

Place an English word of FOUR letters in the empty space. This
word, when added to the end of the three words to the left and to
the beginning of the three words to the right, will form six other
words. What is the word?

ANSWER 13

WORD PUZZLE 81

Place one letter in the middle of this diagram. Four five-letter
words can now be rearranged from each straight line of letters.
What is the letter and what are the words?

ANSWER 54

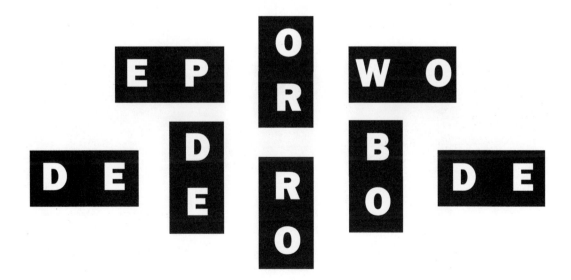

WORD PUZZLE 82

Arrange the tiles in this diagram so that they form a square.
When this is done correctly four words can be read down and
across. What are the words?

ANSWER 2

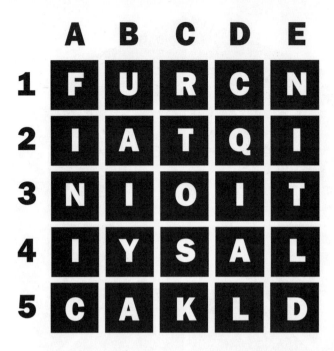

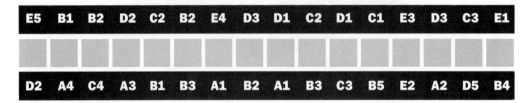

WORD PUZZLE 83

Select one of the two letters from the grid, in accordance with the
reference shown, and place it in the word frame. When the correct
letters have been chosen a sixteen-letter word can be read.
What is the word?

ANSWER 95

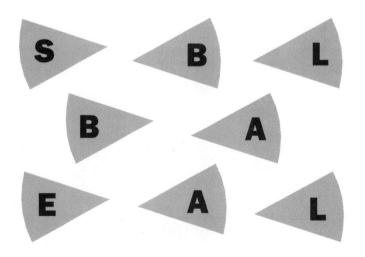

WORD PUZZLE 84

Make a circle out of these shapes.
When the correct circle has been found an English word can be
read clockwise. What is the word?

ANSWER 43

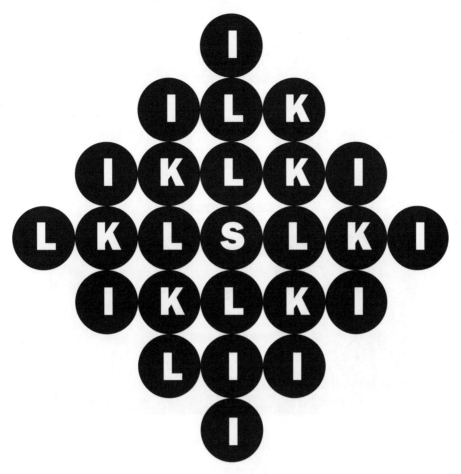

WORD PUZZLE 85

Move from circle to touching circle collecting the letters of SILK.
Always start at the S.
How many different ways are there to do this?

ANSWER 84

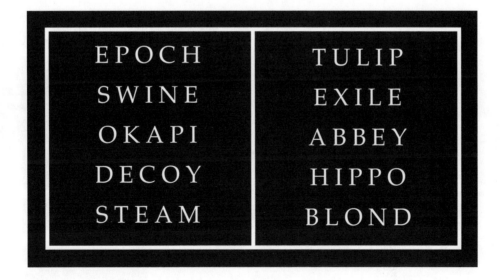

WORD PUZZLE 86

Five of the words in the diagram are associated for some
reason. Find the words and then work out whether FLUTE belongs
to the group.

ANSWER 32

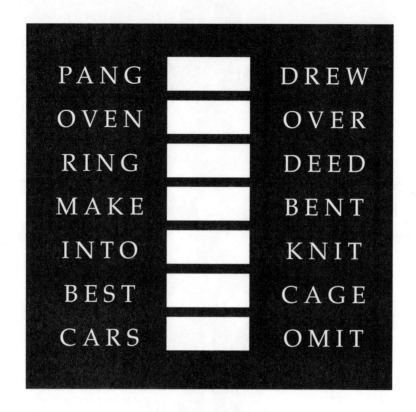

WORD PUZZLE 87

Change the first letter of each word to the left and the right. Two other English words must be formed. Place the letter used in the empty section. When this has been completed for all the words another English word can be read downwards. What is the word?

ANSWER 74

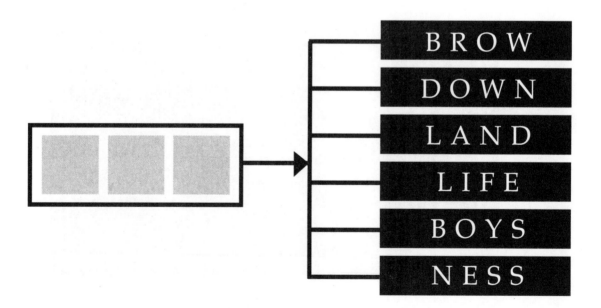

WORD PUZZLE 88

Which English word of three letters can be attached to the front of the words shown in the diagram to create six other words?

ANSWER 22

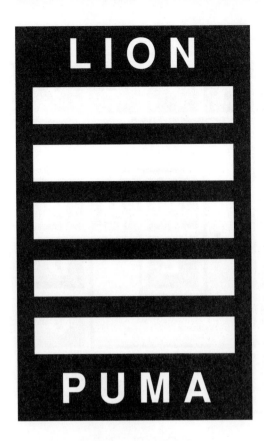

WORD PUZZLE 89

Complete the word ladder by changing one letter of each word
per step. The newly created word must be found in the dictionary.
What are the words to turn LION to PUMA?

ANSWER 64

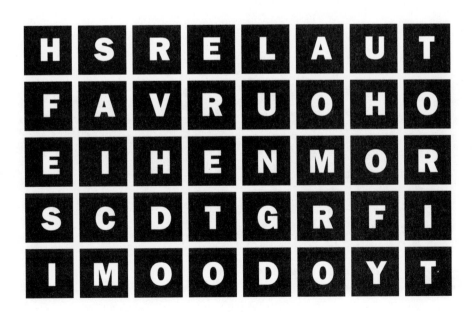

WORD PUZZLE 90

A quotation has been written in this diagram. Find the start letter
and move from square to touching square until you have found it.
What is the quotation and to whom is it attributed?

ANSWER 12

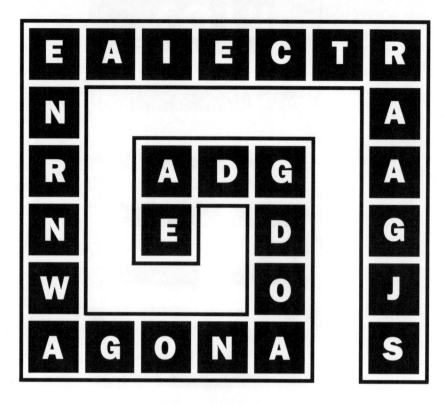

WORD PUZZLE 91

The names of three trees are to be found in the diagram.
The letters of the names are in the order they normally appear.
What are the trees?

ANSWER 53

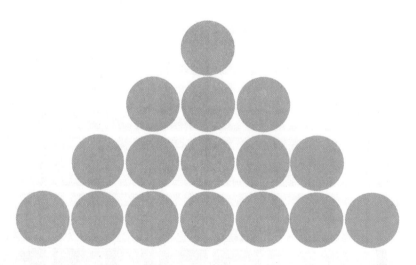

CDEHMNOOOOPPRSST

WORD PUZZLE 92

Place the letters shown into the diagram in such a way
that three words can be read across and one down the middle.
What are the words?

ANSWER 1

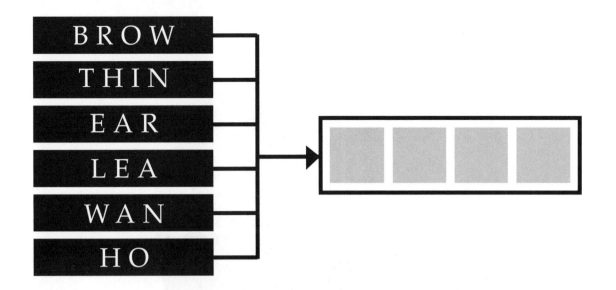

WORD PUZZLE 93

Which English word of four letters can be attached to the back of
the words shown in the diagram to create six other words?

ANSWER 42

WORD PUZZLE 94

Start at the bottom letter A and move from circle to touching circle
to the E at the top right. How many different ways are there of
collecting the nine letters of ABORIGINE?

ANSWER 94

WORD PUZZLE 95

Select one letter from each of the segments.
When the correct letters have been found a word of eight letters
can be read clockwise. What is the word?

ANSWER 83

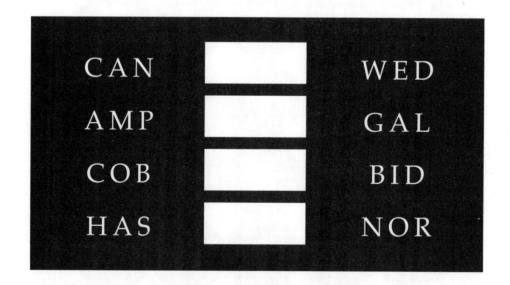

WORD PUZZLE 96

Place two letters in the empty space which, when added to the
end of the words to the left and to the beginning of the right, form
other English words. When this is completed another word
can be read down. What is the word?

ANSWER 31

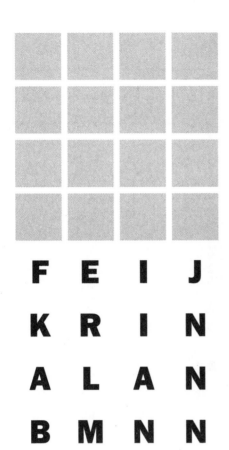

F E I J

K R I N

A L A N

B M N N

WORD PUZZLE 97

Take the letters and arrange
them correctly in the column
under which they appear.
Once this has been done a famous
person will appear.
Who is the person?

ANSWER 73

THE PROFESSIONAL WRESTLER

WAS OF • • • • • • BUILD AND

BORE A • • • • • • AGAINST

HIS OPPONENT.

WORD PUZZLE 98

Two words using the same letters in their construction can be used
to replace the dots in this sentence. The sentence will then make
sense. Each dot is one letter. What are the words?

ANSWER 21

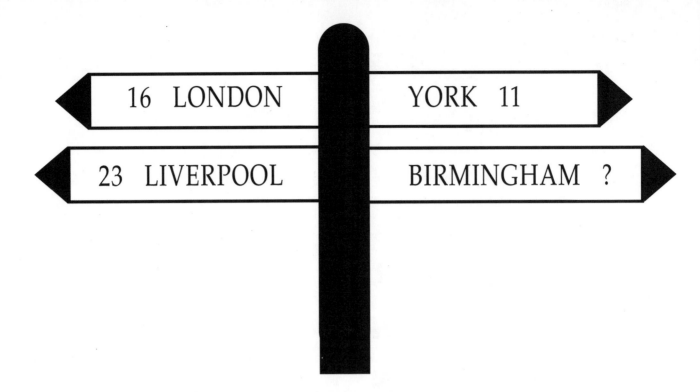

WORD PUZZLE 99

The distances on this signpost are fictitious. They bear a relationship to the letters in the names.
What should replace the question mark?

ANSWER 63

WORD PUZZLE 100

Place an English word of FOUR letters in the empty space. This
word, when added to the end of the three words to the left and to
the beginning of the three words to the right, will form six other
words. What is the word?

ANSWER 11

RED WORD PUZZLE 1

The tiles in this grid have the letters of the word APE
written upon them. Take any three and arrange them
to form the word. Count that as one. Now find
another pattern and count that as two.
How many different patterns can be found?

ANSWER 1 ON LAST PAGE OF THIS SECTION

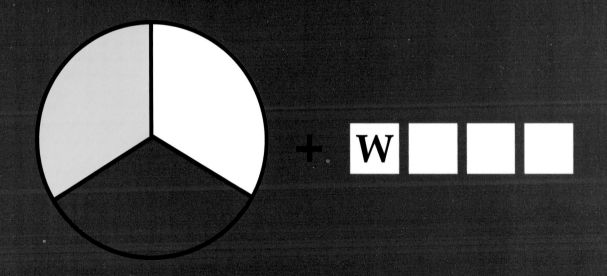

RED WORD PUZZLE 2

The hues in the sphere are a clue to the words. The second part of
each word begins with the letter given
and has one letter per blank shown.
What are the words?

ANSWER 5 ON LAST PAGE OF THIS SECTION

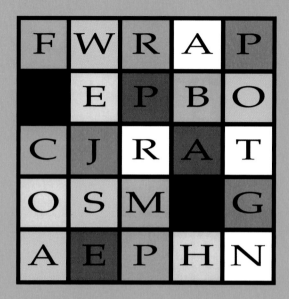

GREEN WORD PUZZLE 1

The word frame at the top is constructed from multi-tinted tiles.
Choose a letter from the grid and insert it in the frame. The letter
must be written on a matching tile. When the process
has been completed a modern ruler can be found.
Who is it?

ANSWER 1 ON LAST PAGE OF THIS SECTION

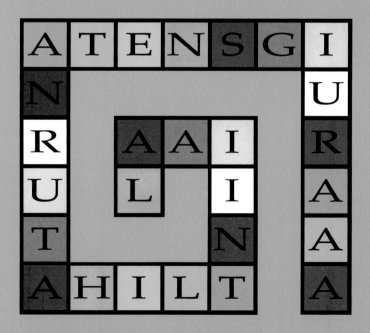

GREEN WORD PUZZLE 2

Three countries can be found
in the diagram. The letters are
written in the correct order.
Only three different shades
of letter are used in each name.
What are the countries?

ANSWER 5 ON LAST PAGE OF THIS
SECTION

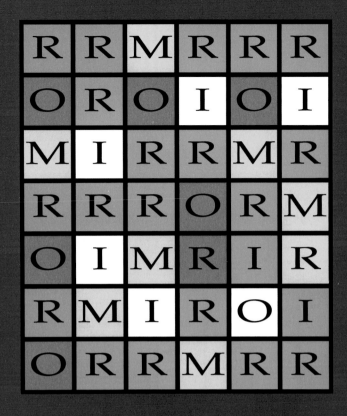

RED WORD PUZZLE 3

Divide the diagram up, using the same shape each time,
in such a way that MIRROR can be read seven times. No two
versions of MIRROR will be alike and they will not overlap.

ANSWER 2 ON LAST PAGE OF THIS SECTION

RED WORD PUZZLE 4

When the correct eight segments are rearranged to form a circle
both a symmetrical pattern and an eight-letter word will be found.
Yellow segments represent A, E, O, and U. Blue segments
represent N, R, S, and V. White segments represent D, I, M, and P.
Green segments represent C, F, H, and T.
What is the word?

ANSWER 6 ON LAST PAGE OF THIS SECTION

BLUE WORD PUZZLE 1

Fill the diagram up with the circles. The black circle goes in the middle and represents the letter W. Red circles are Ss, blue circles are Is, and yellows circles are Es. When the correct pattern has been found, by moving from circle to touching circle, in each case starting at the black circle, the letters of the word WISE can be traced 20 times. What does the pattern look like?

ANSWER 1 ON LAST PAGE OF THIS SECTION

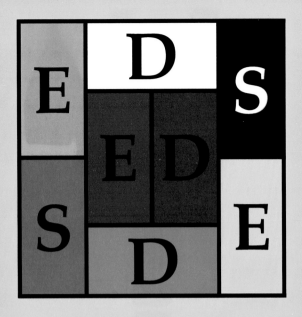

YELLOW WORD PUZZLE 1

The tiles in this grid have the letters of the word DEEDS
written upon them. Take any five and arrange them
to form the word. Count that as one. Now find
another pattern and count that as two.
How many different patterns can be found?

ANSWER 1 ON LAST PAGE OF THIS SECTION

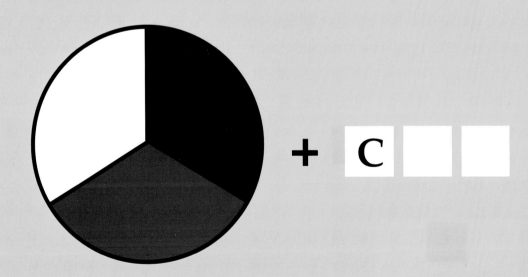

YELLOW WORD PUZZLE 2

The hues in the sphere are a clue to the words. The second
part of each word begins with the letter given
and has one letter per blank shown.
What are the words?

ANSWER 5 ON LAST PAGE OF THIS SECTION

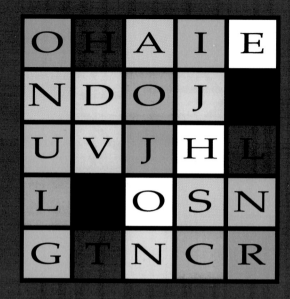

RED WORD PUZZLE 5

The word frame at the top is constructed from multi-tinted tiles.
Choose a letter from the grid and insert it in the frame.
The letter must be written on a matching tile.
When the process has been completed
a fictional character can be found.
Who is it?

ANSWER 3 ON LAST PAGE OF THIS SECTION

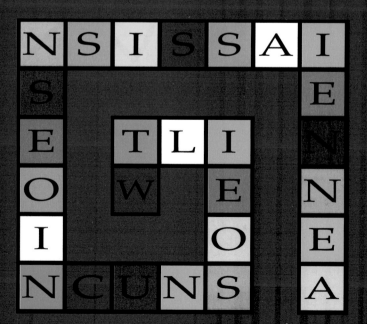

RED WORD PUZZLE 6

Three American States can be found
in the diagram. The letters are
written in the correct order.
Only three different shades
of letter are used in each name.
What are the States?

ANSWER 7 ON LAST PAGE OF THIS
SECTION

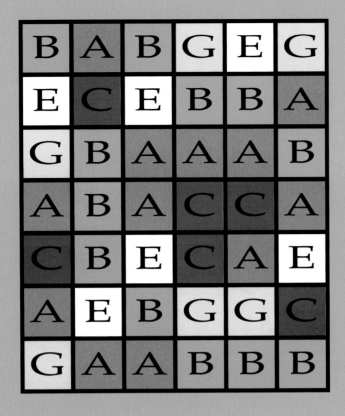

GREEN WORD PUZZLE 3

Divide the diagram up, using the same shape each time,
in such a way that CABBAGE can be read six times. No two
versions of CABBAGE will be alike and they will not overlap.

ANSWER 2 ON LAST PAGE OF THIS SECTION

GREEN WORD PUZZLE 4

When the correct eight segments are rearranged to form a circle
both a symmetrical pattern and an eight-letter word will be found.
Yellowsegments represent either D, M, N, and Y. Blue segments
represent I, K, S, and W. Red segments represent either A, C, H,
and R. White segments represent E, G, O, and U.
What is the word?

ANSWER 6 ON LAST PAGE OF THIS SECTION

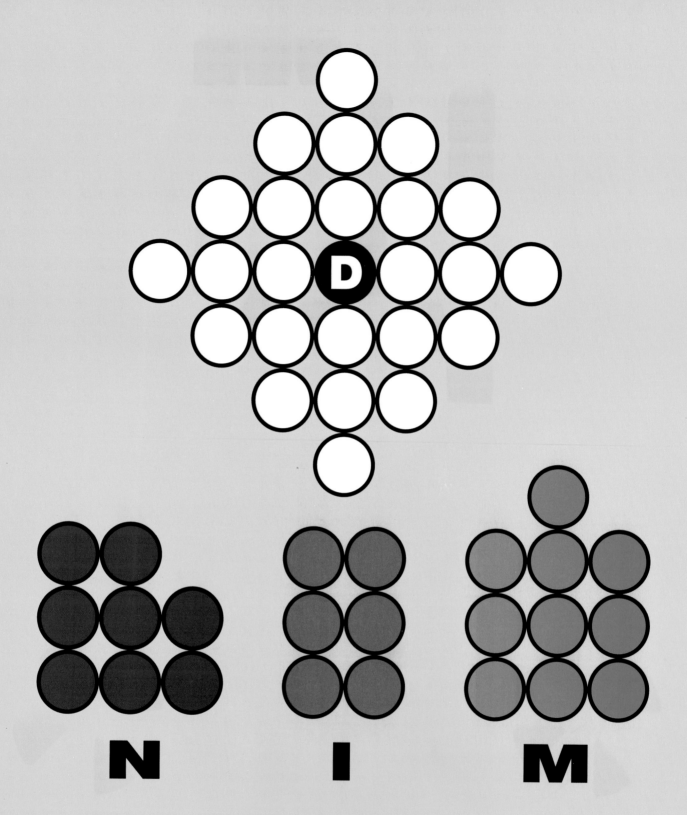

YELLOW WORD PUZZLE 3

Fill the diagram up with the circles. The black circle goes in the middle and represents the letter D. Red circles are Ns, blue circles are Is, and green circles are Ms. When the correct pattern has been found, by moving from circle to touching circle, in each case starting at the black circle, the letters of the word MIND can be traced 11 times. What does the pattern look like?

ANSWER 2 ON LAST PAGE OF THIS SECTION

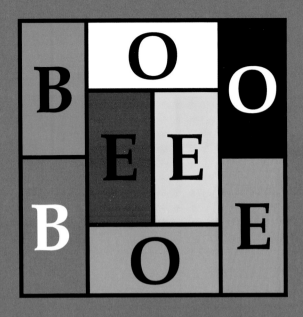

BLUE WORD PUZZLE 2

The tiles in this grid have the letters of the word OBOE
written upon them. Take any four and arrange
them to form the word. Count that as one.
Now find another pattern and count that as two.
How many different patterns can be found?

ANSWER 2 ON LAST PAGE OF THIS SECTION

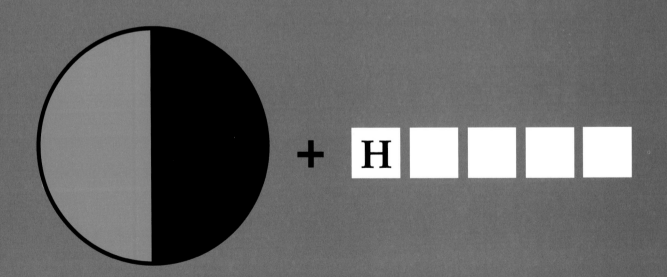

BLUE WORD PUZZLE 3

The hues in the sphere are a clue to the words. The second part of
each word begins with the letter given
and has one letter per blank shown.
What are the words?

ANSWER 4 ON LAST PAGE OF THIS SECTION

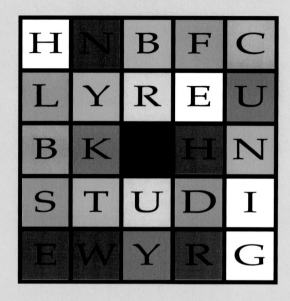

YELLOW WORD PUZZLE 4

The word frame at the top is constructed from multi-tinted tiles.
Choose a letter from the grid and insert it in the frame.
The letter must be written on a matching tile.
When the process has been completed
a fictional character can be found.
Who is it?

ANSWER 3 ON LAST PAGE OF THIS SECTION

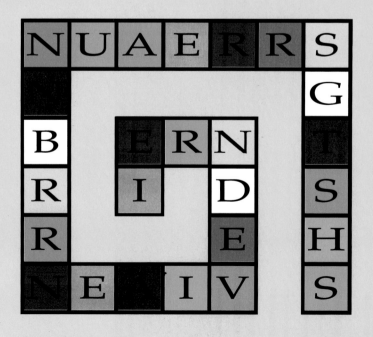

YELLOW WORD PUZZLE 5

Three Scottish Towns can be found in the diagram. The letters are written in the correct order. Only three different shades of letter are used in each name. What are the towns?

ANSWER 6 ON LAST PAGE OF THIS SECTION

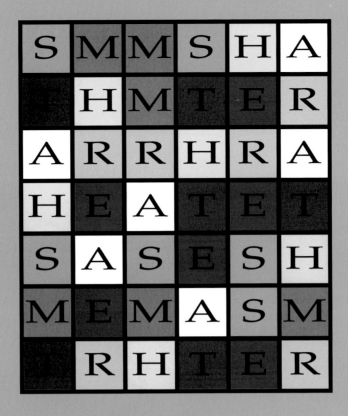

GREEN WORD PUZZLE 5

Divide the diagram up, using the same shape each time,
in such a way that HAMSTER can be read six times.
No two HAMSTER will be alike and they will not overlap.

ANSWER 3 ON LAST PAGE OF THIS SECTION

GREEN WORD PUZZLE 6

When the correct eight segments are rearranged to form a circle
both a symmetrical pattern and an eight-letter word will be found.
Yellow segments represent A, E, G, and L. Blue segments
represent B, I, O, and V. White segments represent H, R, T, and U.
Red segments represent K, P, Q, and Y.
What is the word?

ANSWER 7 ON LAST PAGE OF THIS SECTION

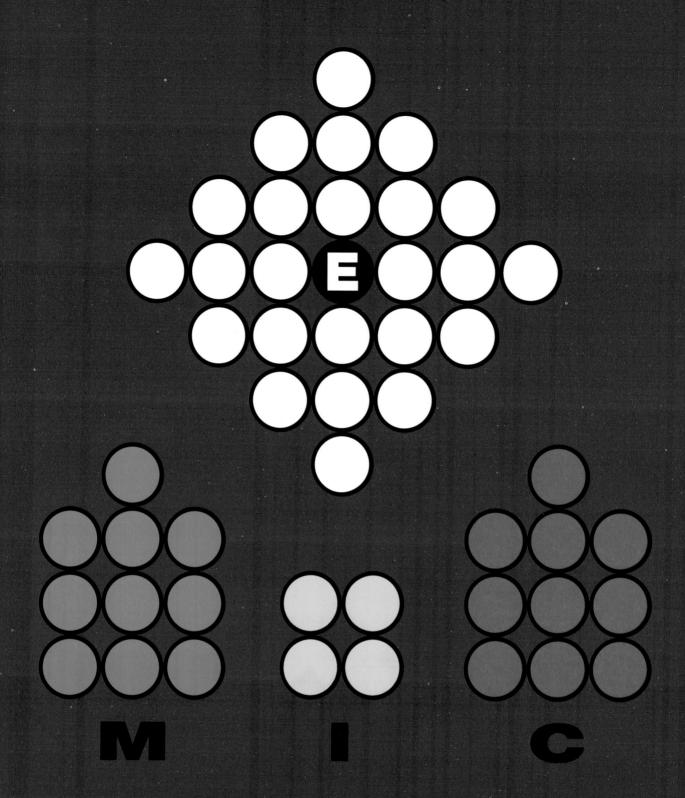

RED WORD PUZZLE 7

Fill the diagram up with the circles. The black circle goes in the middle and represents the letter E. Yellow circles are Is, blue circles are Cs, and Green circles are Ms. When the correct pattern has been found, by moving from circle to touching circle, in each case starting at the black circle, the letters of the word MICE can be traced 18 times. What does the pattern look like?

ANSWER 4 ON LAST PAGE OF THIS SECTION

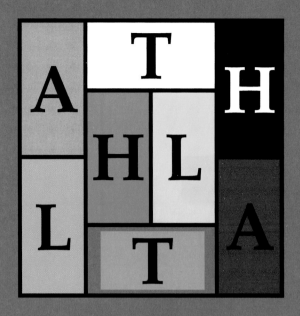

BLUE WORD PUZZLE 4

The tiles in this grid have the letters of the word HALT
written upon them. Take any four and arrange them
to form the word. Count that as one. Now find
another pattern and count that as two.
How many different patterns can be found?

ANSWER 3 ON LAST PAGE OF THIS SECTION

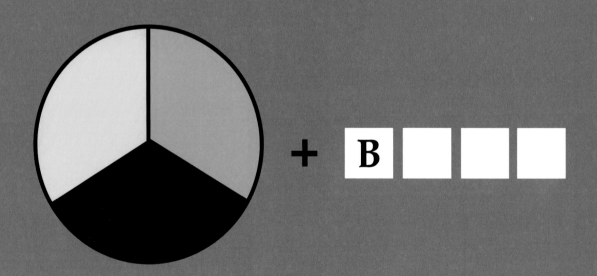

BLUE WORD PUZZLE 5

The hues in the sphere are a clue to the words. The second
part of each word begins with the letter given
and has one letter per blank shown.
What are the words?

ANSWER 5 ON LAST PAGE OF THIS SECTION

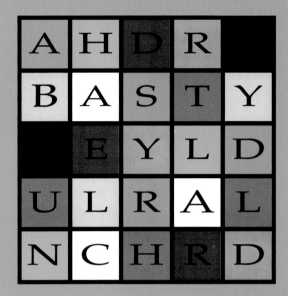

GREEN WORD PUZZLE 7

The word frame at the top is constructed from multi-tinted tiles.
Choose a letter from the grid and insert it in the frame.
The letter must be written on a matching tile.
When the process has been completed two film
stars can be found.
Who are they?

ANSWER 4 ON LAST PAGE OF THIS SECTION

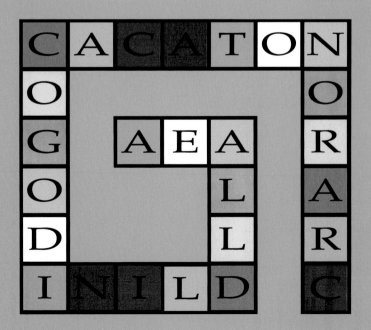

GREEN WORD PUZZLE 8

Three reptiles can be found
in the diagram. The letters are
written in the correct order.
Only three different shades
of letter are used in each name.
What are they?

ANSWER 8 ON LAST PAGE OF THIS
SECTION

YELLOW WORD PUZZLE 6

Divide the diagram up, using the same shape each time,
in such a way that LACQUER can be read six times.
No two LACQUER will be alike and they will not overlap.

ANSWER 4 ON LAST PAGE OF THIS SECTION

YELLOW WORD PUZZLE 7

When the correcteight segments are rearranged to form a circle
both a symmetrical pattern and an eight-letter word will be found.
Green segments represent either I, K, O, and S. Blue segments
represent B, O, R, and T. Red segments represent either D, J, L,
and M. White segments represent C, E, U, and Y.
What is the word?

ANSWER 7 ON LAST PAGE OF THIS SECTION

Red Word Puzzles

1. 12.

2.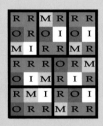

3. Long John Silver.

4.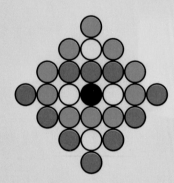

5. Orangewood, Redwood and Whitewood.

6. Ancestor.

7. Wisconsin, Tennessee and Louisiana.

Green Word Puzzles

1. Emperor of Japan.

2.

3.

4. Laurel and Hardy..

5. Argentina, Australia and Lithuania.

6. Rickshaw.

7. Laughter.

8. Crocodile, Alligator and Anaconda.

Blue Word Puzzles

1.

2. 36.

3. 16.

4. Greenheart and Blackheart.

5. Blackbird, Bluebird and Yellowbird.

Yellow Word Puzzles

1. 72.

2.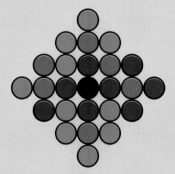

3. Huckleberry Finn.

4.

5. Redcap, Whitecap and Blackcap.

6. Edinburgh, Inverness and Stranraer.

7. Courtesy.

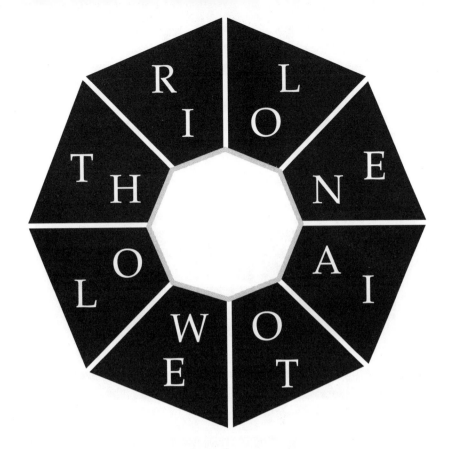

WORD PUZZLE 101

Place one letter in the middle of this diagram. Four five-letter
words can now be rearranged from each straight line of letters.
What is the letter and what are the words?

ANSWER 52

WORD PUZZLE 102

Arrange the tiles in this diagram so that they form a square.
When this is done correctly five words can be read downwards
and across. What are the words?

ANSWER 104

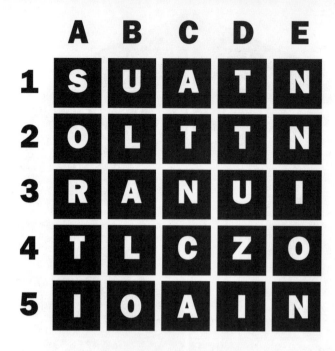

	A	B	C	D	E
1	S	U	A	T	N
2	O	L	T	T	N
3	R	A	N	U	I
4	T	L	C	Z	O
5	I	O	A	I	N

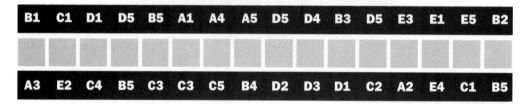

B1	C1	D1	D5	B5	A1	A4	A5	D5	D4	B3	D5	E3	E1	E5	B2
A3	E2	C4	B5	C3	C3	C5	B4	D2	D3	D1	C2	A2	E4	C1	B5

WORD PUZZLE 103

Select one of the two letters from the grid, in accordance with the
reference shown, and place it in the word frame. When the correct
letters have been chosen a sixteen-letter word can be read.
What is the word?

ANSWER 93

WORD PUZZLE 104

Make a circle out of these shapes.
When the correct circle has been found an English word can be
read clockwise. What is the word?

ANSWER 41

WORD PUZZLE 105

Move from circle to touching circle collecting the letters of FISH.
Always start at the F.
How many different ways are there to do this?

ANSWER 167

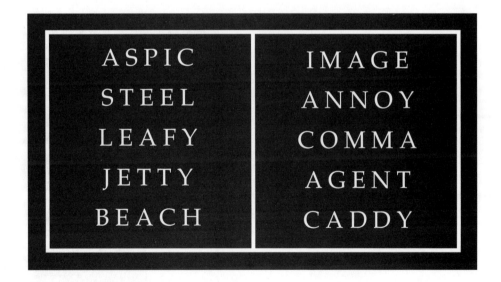

WORD PUZZLE 106

Five of the words in the diagram are associated for some
reason. Find the words and then work out whether CHEER
belongs to the group.

ANSWER 115

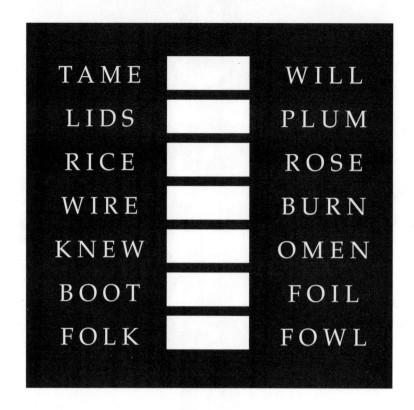

TAME		WILL
LIDS		PLUM
RICE		ROSE
WIRE		BURN
KNEW		OMEN
BOOT		FOIL
FOLK		FOWL

WORD PUZZLE 107

Change the first letter of each word to the left and the right. Two other English words must be formed. Place the letter used in the empty section. When this has been completed for all the words another English word can be read down. What is the word?

ANSWER 134

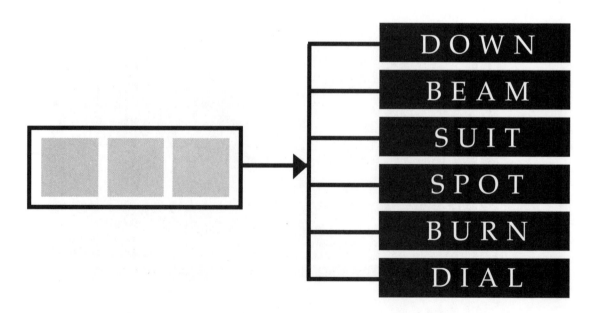

DOWN

BEAM

SUIT

SPOT

BURN

DIAL

WORD PUZZLE 108

Which English word of three letters can be attached to the front of the words shown in the diagram to create six other words?

ANSWER 156

WORD PUZZLE 109

Complete the word ladder by changing one letter of each word
per step. The newly created word must be found in the dictionary.
What are the words to turn BLAZE to GLORY?

ANSWER 197

WORD PUZZLE 110

A quotation has been written in this diagram. Find the start letter
and move from square to touching square until you have found it.
What is the quotation and to whom is it attributed?

ANSWER 145

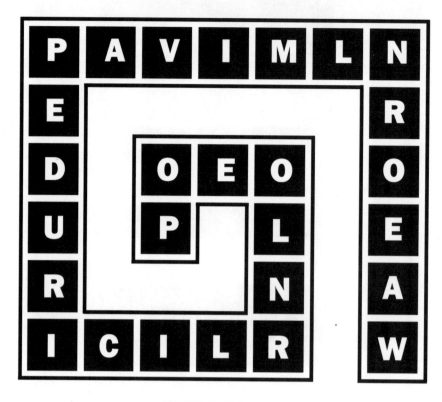

WORD PUZZLE 111

The names of three animals are to be found in the diagram.
The letters of the names are in the order they normally appear.
What are the animals?

ANSWER 166

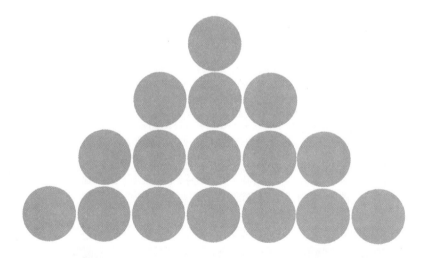

A A A E E I M M N N N O R R S T

WORD PUZZLE 112

Place the letters shown into the diagram in such a way
that three words can be read across and one down the middle.
What are the words?

ANSWER 114

WORD PUZZLE 113

Start at the bottom letter F and move from circle to touching circle to the S at the top right. How many different ways are there of collecting the nine letters of FESTIVALS ?

ANSWER 125

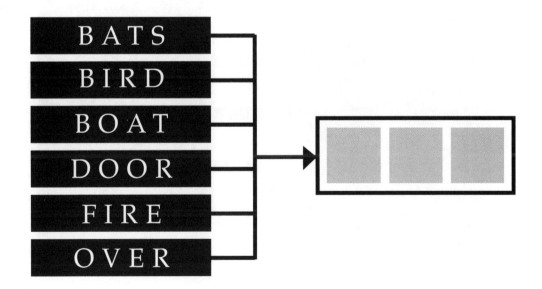

WORD PUZZLE 114

Which English word of three letters can be attached to the back of the words shown in the diagram to create six other words?

ANSWER 155

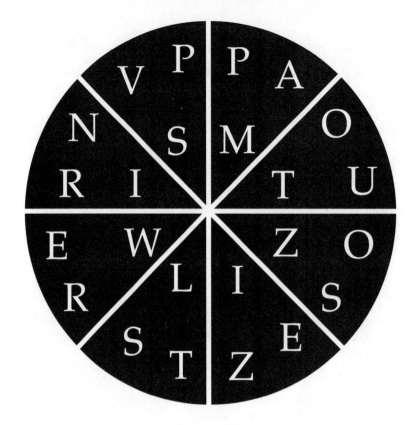

WORD PUZZLE 115

Select one letter from each of the segments.
When the correct letters have been found a word of eight letters
can be read clockwise. What is the word?

ANSWER 196

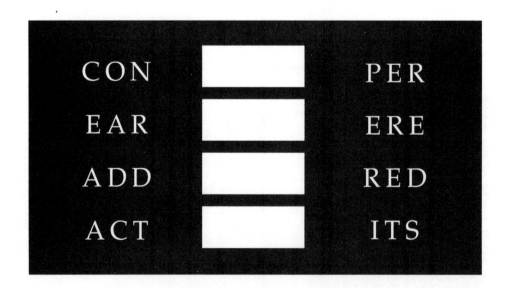

WORD PUZZLE 116

Place two letters in the empty space which, when added to the
end of the words to the left and to the beginning of the right, form
other English words. When this is completed another word
can be read down. What is the word?

ANSWER 144

H O R C

T I N S

W U L L

H I N C

WORD PUZZLE 117

Take the letters and arrange
them correctly in the column
under which they appear.
Once this has been done the name
of a famous person will emerge.
What is the name ?

ANSWER 186

WORD PUZZLE 118

Start at the bottom letter F and move from circle to touching circle
to the N at the top right. How many different ways are there of collecting the nine letters of FISHERMAN?

ANSWER 177

PIZZA	78
BURGER	71
STEAK	56
FRIES	?

WORD PUZZLE 119

On this list of stock the number of packets of each food are written
. The numbers bear a relationship to the letters in the words. What
should replace the question mark?

ANSWER 176

WORD PUZZLE 120

Place an English word of THREE letters in the empty space. This
word, when added to the end of the three words to the left and to
the beginning of the three words to the right, will form six other
words. What is the word?

ANSWER 124

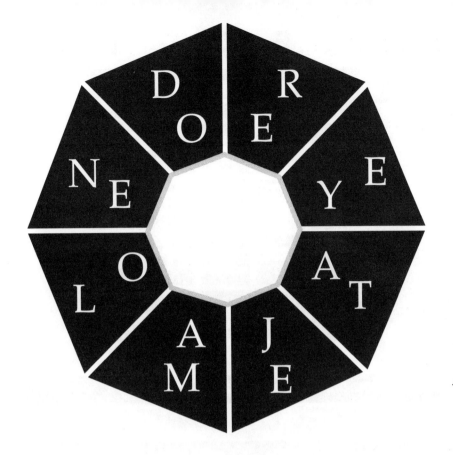

WORD PUZZLE 121

Place one letter in the middle of this diagram. Four five-letter
words can now be rearranged from each straight line of letters.
What is the letter and what are the words?

ANSWER 165

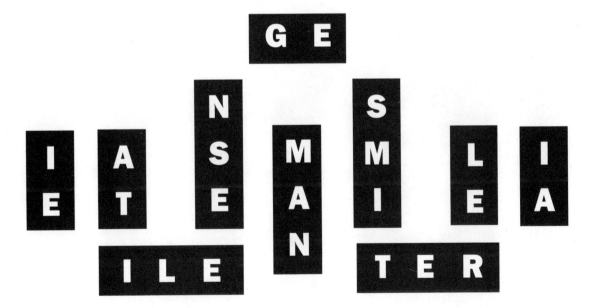

WORD PUZZLE 122

Arrange the tiles in this diagram so that they form a square.
When this is done correctly five words can be read downwards
and across. What are the words?

ANSWER 113

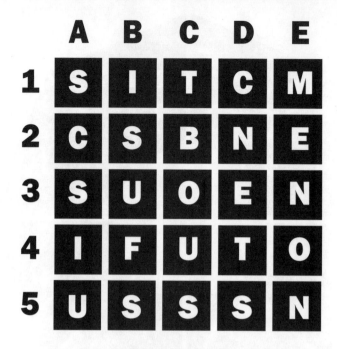

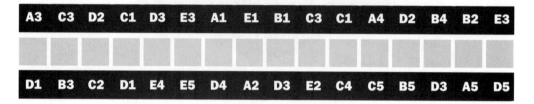

WORD PUZZLE 123

Select one of the two letters from the grid, in accordance with the reference shown, and place it in the word frame. When the correct letters have been chosen a sixteen-letter word can be read.
What is the word?

ANSWER 206

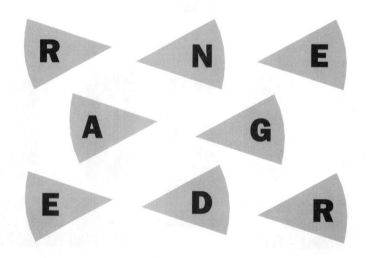

WORD PUZZLE 124

Make a circle out of these shapes.
When the correct circle has been found an English word can be read clockwise. What is the word?

ANSWER 154

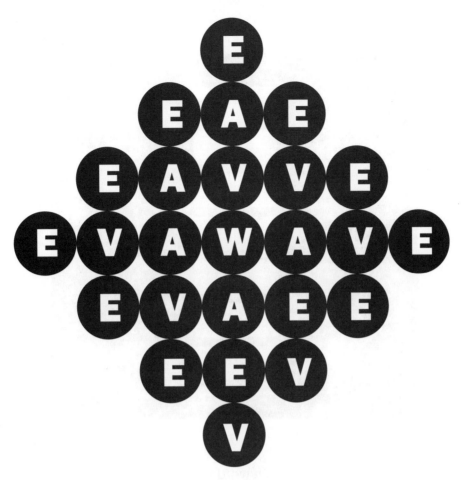

WORD PUZZLE 125

Move from circle to touching circle collecting the letters of WAVE.
Always start at the W.
How many different ways are there to do this?

ANSWER 195

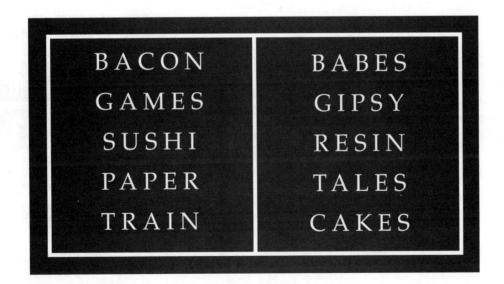

WORD PUZZLE 126

Five of the words in the diagram are associated for some
reason. Find the words and then work out whether CAFES belongs
to the group.

ANSWER 143

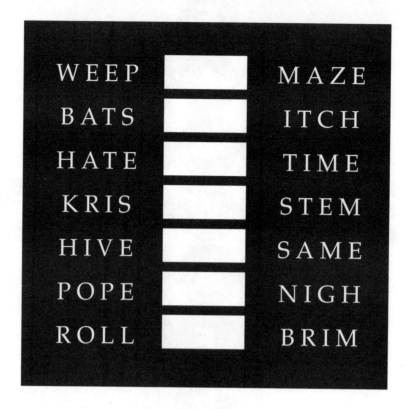

WEEP		MAZE
BATS		ITCH
HATE		TIME
KRIS		STEM
HIVE		SAME
POPE		NIGH
ROLL		BRIM

WORD PUZZLE 127

Change the first letter of each word to the left and the right. Two other English words must be formed. Place the letter used in the empty section. When this has been completed for all the words another English word can be read down. What is the word?

ANSWER 185

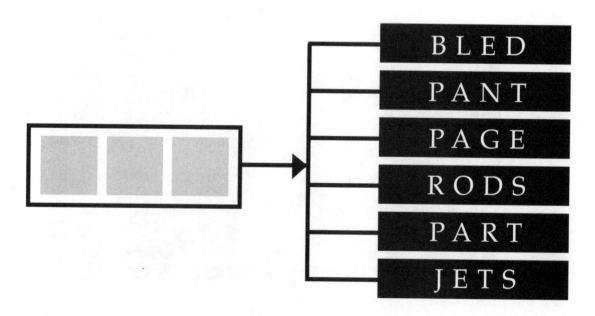

BLED

PANT

PAGE

RODS

PART

JETS

WORD PUZZLE 128

Which English word of three letters can be attached to the front of the words shown in the diagram to create six other words?

ANSWER 133

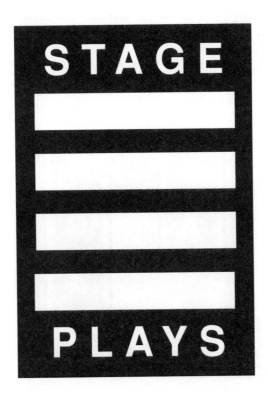

WORD PUZZLE 129

Complete the word ladder by changing one letter of each word
per step. The newly created word must be found in the dictionary.
What are the words to turn STAGE to PLAYS?

ANSWER 175

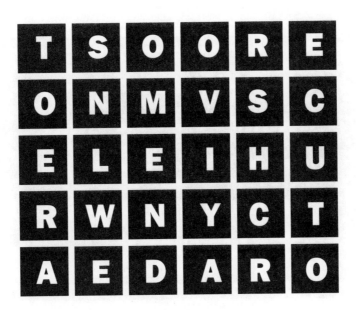

WORD PUZZLE 130

A quotation has been written in this diagram. Find the start letter
and move from square to touching square until you have found it.
What is the quotation and to whom is it attributed?

ANSWER 123

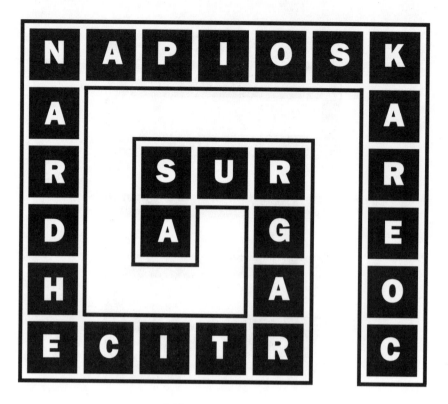

WORD PUZZLE 131

The names of three plants are to be found in the diagram.
The letters of the names are in the order they normally appear.
What are theplants?

ANSWER 164

IN THE FOREST AS THE

FRUIT • • • • • • THE

FURTIVE • • • • • • LURKS

IN ANTICIPATION OF

HIS VICTIM.

WORD PUZZLE 132

Two words using the same letters in their construction can be used
to replace the dots in this sentence. The sentence will then make
sense. Each dot is one letter. What are the words?

ANSWER 112

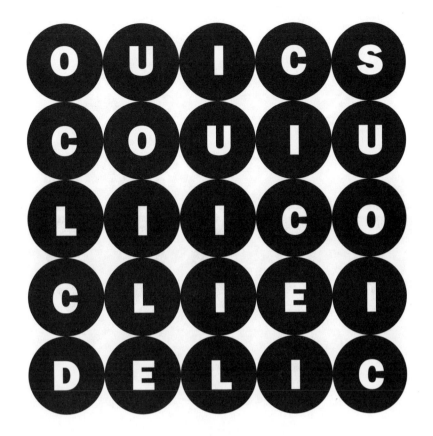

WORD PUZZLE 133

Start at the bottom letter D and move from circle to touching circle to the S at the top right. How many different ways are there of collecting the nine letters of DELICIOUS?

ANSWER 205

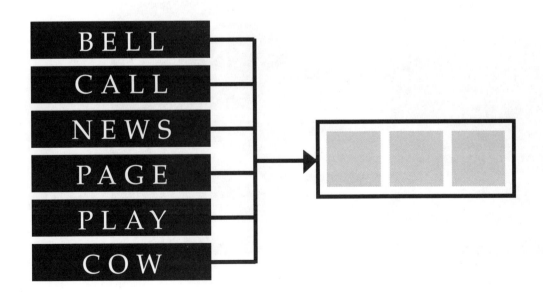

WORD PUZZLE 134

Which English word of three letters can be attached to the back of the words shown in the diagram to create six other words?

ANSWER 153

WORD PUZZLE 135

Select one letter from each of the segments.
When the correct letters have been found a word of eight letters
can be read clockwise. What is the word?

ANSWER 194

WORD PUZZLE 136

Place two letters in the empty space which, when added to the
end of the words to the left and to the beginning of the right, form
other English words.
When this is completed another word can be read down. What is
the word?

S E O N
G H O R
G T W A
G E I N

WORD PUZZLE 137

Take the letters and arrange
them correctly in the column
under which they appear.
Once this has been done the name
of a famous person will emerge.
What is the name?

ANSWER 184

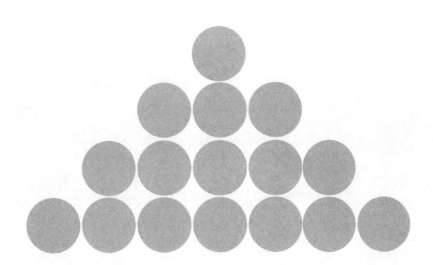

A A A B C D D E H I K L M N R Y

WORD PUZZLE 138

Place the letters shown into the diagram in such a way
that three words can be read across and one down the middle.
What are the words?

ANSWER 132

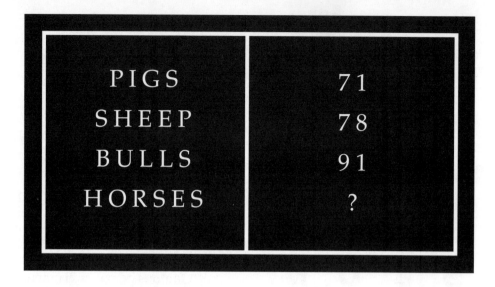

WORD PUZZLE 139

On this list of farm stock the number of animals is written. The numbers bear a relationship to the letters in the words. What should replace the question mark?

ANSWER 174

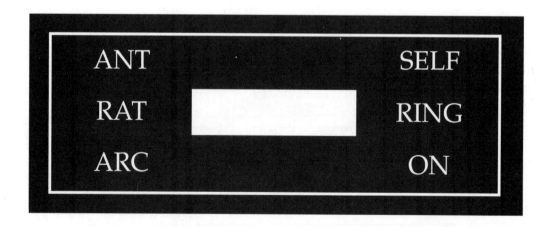

WORD PUZZLE 140

Place an English word of THREE letters in the empty space. This word, when added to the end of the three words to the left and to the beginning of the three words to the right, will form six other words. What is the word?

ANSWER 122

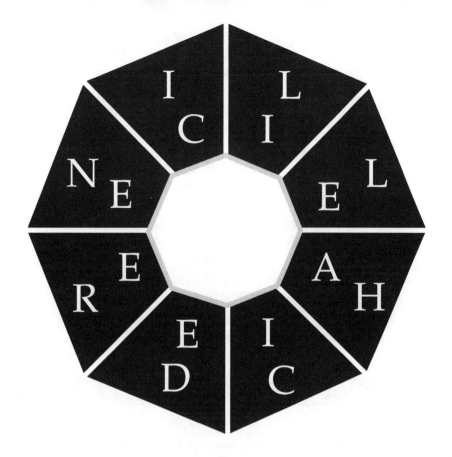

WORD PUZZLE 141

Place one letter in the middle of this diagram. Four five-letter
words can now be rearranged from each straight line of letters.
What is the letter and what are the words?

ANSWER 163

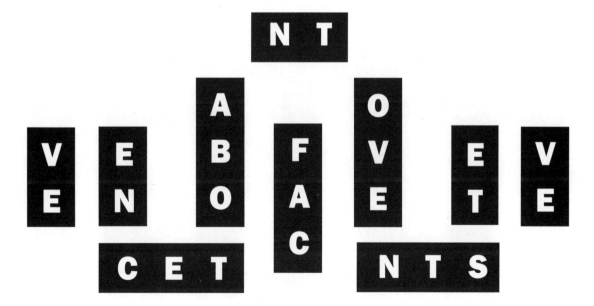

WORD PUZZLE 142

Arrange the tiles in this diagram so that they form a square.
When this is done correctly five words can be read down and
across. What are the words?

ANSWER 111

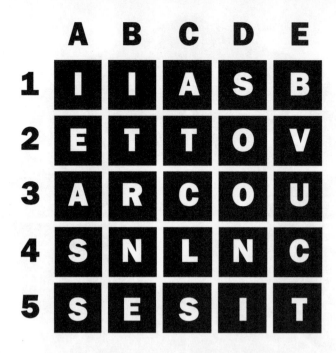

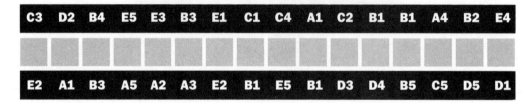

C3	D2	B4	E5	E3	B3	E1	C1	C4	A1	C2	B1	B1	A4	B2	E4
E2	A1	B3	A5	A2	A3	E2	B1	E5	B1	D3	D4	B5	C5	D5	D1

WORD PUZZLE 143

Select one of the two letters from the grid, in accordance with the reference shown, and place it in the word frame. When the correct letters have been chosen a sixteen-letter word can be read. What is the word?

ANSWER 204

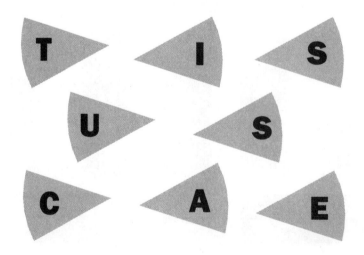

WORD PUZZLE 144

Make a circle out of these shapes.
When the correct circle has been found an English word can be read clockwise. What is the word?

ANSWER 152

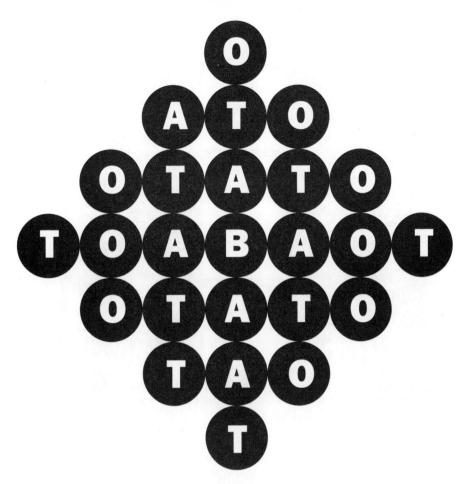

WORD PUZZLE 145

Move from circle to touching circle collecting the letters of BOAT.
Always start at the B.
How many different ways are there to do this?

ANSWER 193

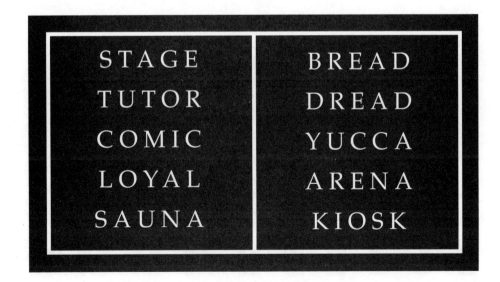

WORD PUZZLE 146

Five of the words in the diagram are associated for some
reason. Find the words and then work out whether WIDOW
belongs to the group.

ANSWER 141

THIN		RAGE
SKIN		FIRS
WIFE		BUMP
SOUR		TANK
DARK		MOST
CHIP		WEAR
WILY		BATH

WORD PUZZLE 147

Change the first letter of each word to the left and the right. Two other English words must be formed. Place the letter used in the empty section. When this has been completed for all the words another English word can be read down. What is the word?

ANSWER 183

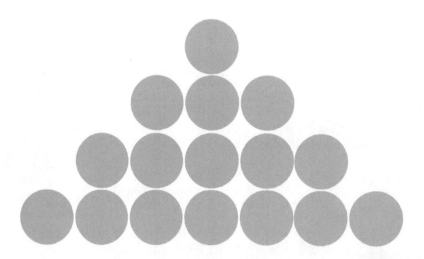

A A A B C E E E H M M M R T T Z

WORD PUZZLE 148

Place the letters shown into the diagram in such a way that three words can be read across and one down the middle. What are the words?

ANSWER 131

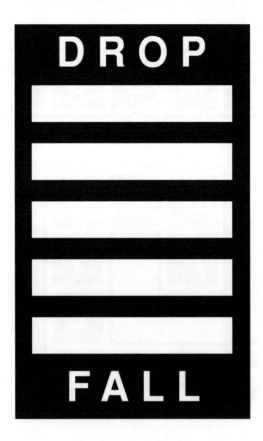

WORD PUZZLE 149

Complete the word ladder by changing one letter of each word
per step. The newly created word must be found in the dictionary.
What are the words to turn DROP to FALL?

ANSWER 173

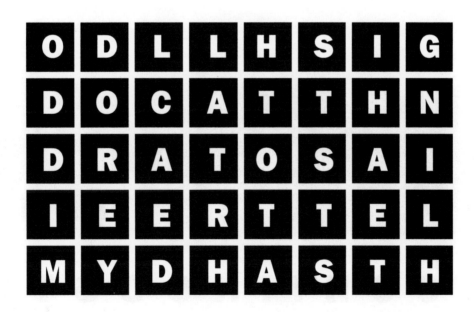

WORD PUZZLE 150

A quotation has been written in this diagram. Find the start letter
and move from square to touching square until you have found it.
What is the quotation and to whom is it attributed?

ANSWER 121

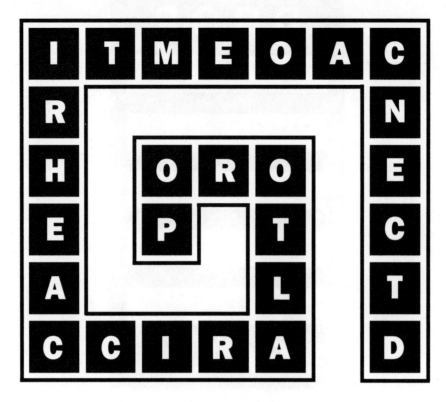

WORD PUZZLE 151

The names of three professions are to be found in the diagram.
The letters of the names are in the order they normally appear.
What are the professions?

ANSWER 162

A B C C C H I I N O O S T T T U

WORD PUZZLE 152

Place the letters shown into the diagram in such a way
that three words can be read across and one down the middle.
What are the words?

ANSWER 110

THE VALUABLE SCIENTIFIC EQUIPMENT WAS CAREFULLY • • • • • • AND CHECKED BEFORE BEING • • • • • • TO THE OTHER SIDE OF THE BUILDING.

WORD PUZZLE 153

Two words using the same letters in their construction can be used to replace the dots in this sentence. The sentence will then make sense. Each dot is one letter. What are the words?

ANSWER 203

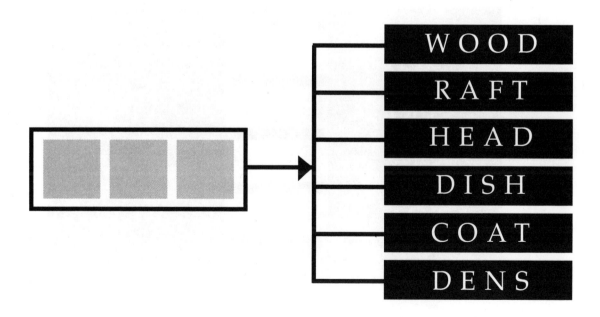

WORD PUZZLE 154

Which English word of three letters can be attached to the front of the words shown in the diagram to create six other words?

ANSWER 151

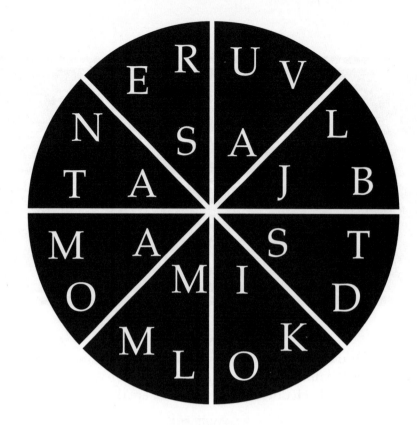

WORD PUZZLE 155

Select one letter from each of the segments.
When the correct letters have been found a word of eight letters
can be read clockwise. What is the word?

ANSWER 192

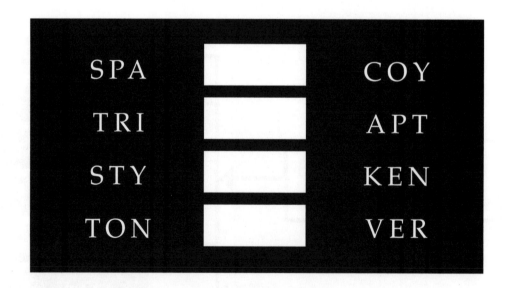

WORD PUZZLE 156

Place two letters in the empty space which, when added to the
end of the words to the left and to the beginning of the right, form
other English words. When this is completed another word
can be read down. What is the word?

ANSWER 140

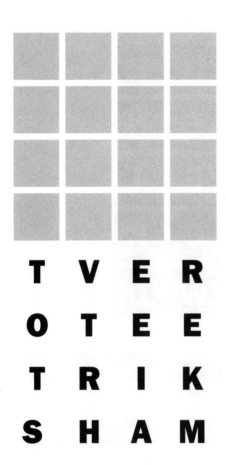

T V E R

O T E E

T R I K

S H A M

WORD PUZZLE 157

Take the letters and arrange
them correctly in the column
under which they appear.
Once this has been done the name
of a film will emerge.
What is it?

ANSWER 182

WORD PUZZLE 158

Arrange the tiles in this diagram so that they form a square.
When this is done correctly five words can be read down and
across. What are the words?

ANSWER 130

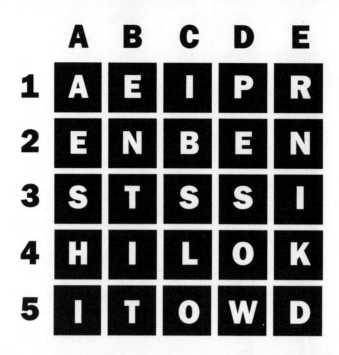

	A	B	C	D	E
1	A	E	I	P	R
2	E	N	B	E	N
3	S	T	S	S	I
4	H	I	L	O	K
5	I	T	O	W	D

E1	A1	E1	B1	D4	B3	A3	A5	D4	E5	C4	E1	D5	D4	D2	E4
D1	A2	C3	D1	B2	E2	A4	C5	C2	C1	D4	B4	B5	E3	E1	D3

WORD PUZZLE 159

Select one of the two letters from the grid, in accordance with the reference shown, and place it in the word frame. When the correct letters have been chosen a sixteen-letter word can be read.
What is the word?

ANSWER 172

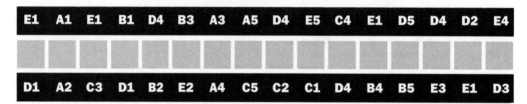

THE LANGUAGE USED BY THE • • • • • • AT THE BASEBALL GAME WAS SO • • • • • • • IT WAS SCARCELY UNDERSTANDABLE.

WORD PUZZLE 160

Two words using the same letters in their construction can be used to replace the dots in this sentence. The sentence will then make sense. Each dot is one letter. What are the words?

ANSWER 120

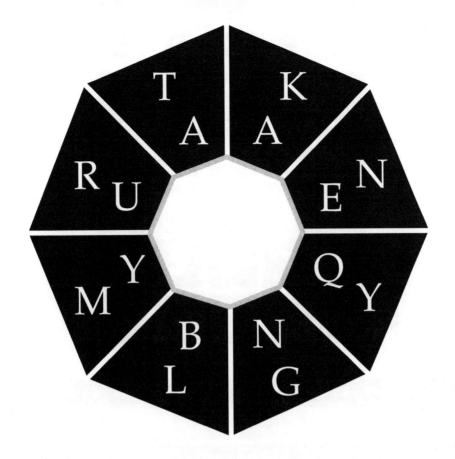

WORD PUZZLE 161

Place one letter in the middle of this diagram. Four five-letter
words can now be rearranged from each straight line of letters.
What is the letter and what are the words?

ANSWER 161

WORD PUZZLE 162

Arrange the tiles in this diagram so that they form a square.
When this is done correctly five words can be read downwards
and across. What are the words?

ANSWER 109

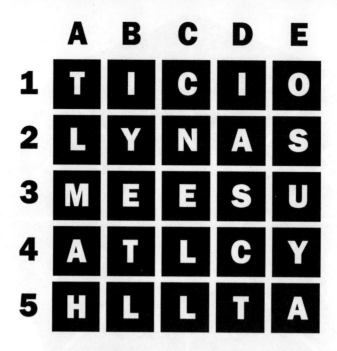

	A	B	C	D	E
1	T	I	C	I	O
2	L	Y	N	A	S
3	M	E	E	S	U
4	A	T	L	C	Y
5	H	L	L	T	A

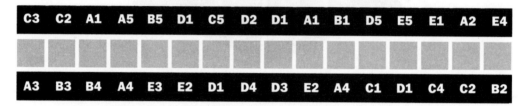

C3	C2	A1	A5	B5	D1	C5	D2	D1	A1	B1	D5	E5	E1	A2	E4
A3	B3	B4	A4	E3	E2	D1	D4	D3	E2	A4	C1	D1	C4	C2	B2

WORD PUZZLE 163

Select one of the two letters from the grid, in accordance with the reference shown, and place it in the word frame. When the correct letters have been chosen a sixteen-letter word can be read.
What is the word?

ANSWER 202

WORD PUZZLE 164

Make a circle out of these shapes.
When the correct circle has been found an English word can be read clockwise. What is the word?

ANSWER 150

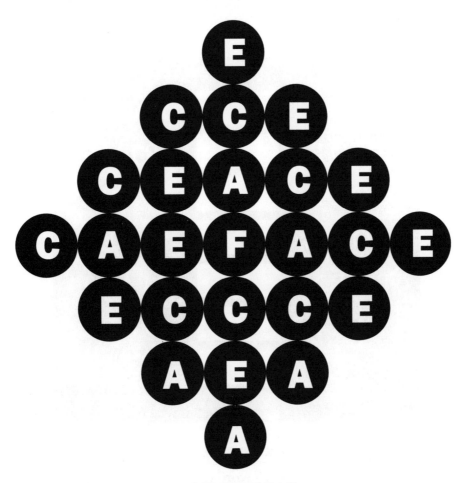

WORD PUZZLE 165

Move from circle to touching circle collecting the letters of FACE.
Always start at the F.
How many different ways are there to do this?

ANSWER 191

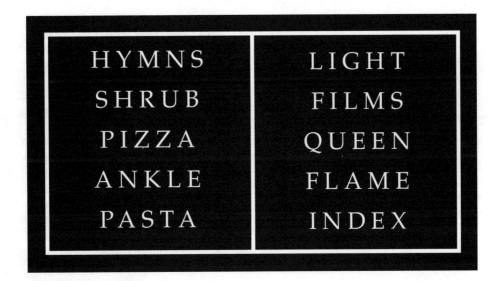

HYMNS   LIGHT

SHRUB   FILMS

PIZZA   QUEEN

ANKLE   FLAME

PASTA   INDEX

WORD PUZZLE 166

Six of the words in the diagram are associated for some
reason. Find the words and then work out whether GLOBE
belongs to the group.

ANSWER 139

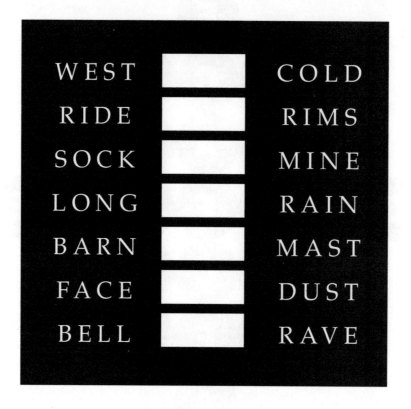

WORD PUZZLE 167

Change the first letter of each word to the left and the right. Two other English words must be formed. Place the letter used in the empty section. When this has been completed for all the words another English word can be read down. What is the word?

ANSWER 181

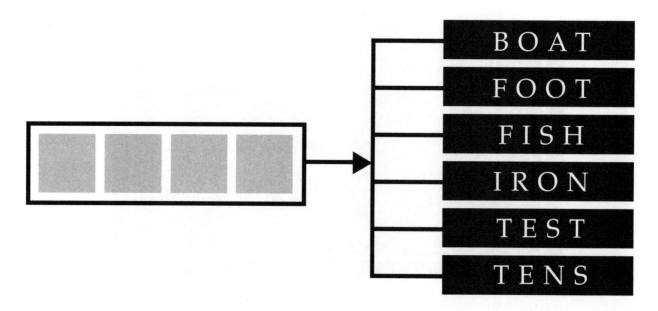

WORD PUZZLE 168

Which English word of four letters can be attached to the front of the words shown in the diagram to create six other words?

ANSWER 129

WORD PUZZLE 169

Complete the word ladder by changing one letter of each word
per step. The newly created word must be found in the dictionary.
What are the words to turn PORT to SHIP?

ANSWER 171

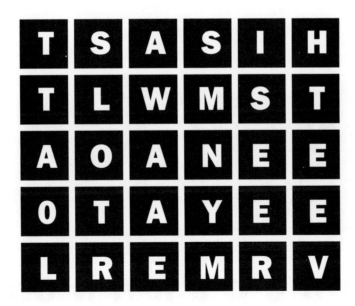

WORD PUZZLE 170

A quotation has been written in this diagram. Find the start letter
and move from square to touching square until you have found it.
What is the quotation and to whom is it attributed?

ANSWER 119

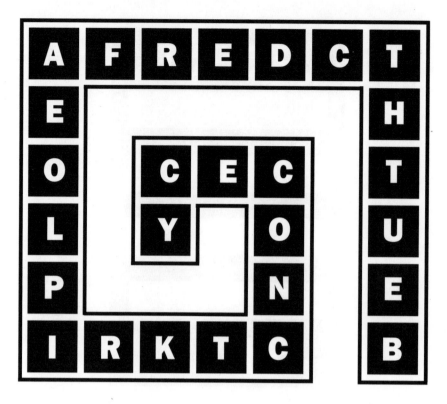

WORD PUZZLE 171

The names of three insects are to be found in the diagram.
The letters of the names are in the order they normally appear.
What are the insects?

ANSWER 160

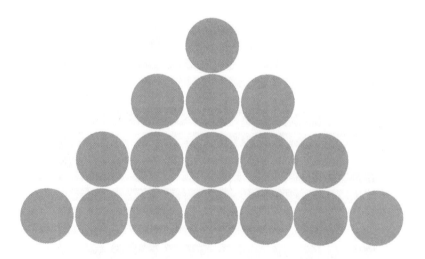

ABAAABCCEHNNOORSST

WORD PUZZLE 172

Place the letters shown into the diagram in such a way
that three words can be read across and one down the middle.
What are the words?

ANSWER 108

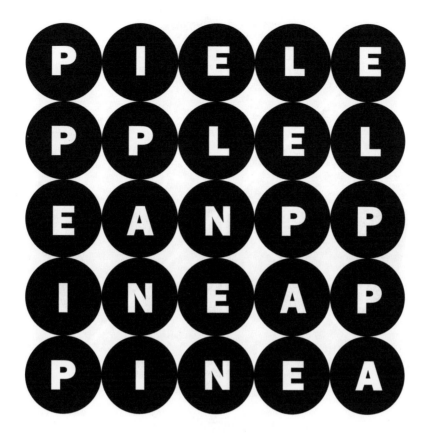

WORD PUZZLE 173

Start at the bottom letter P and move from circle to touching circle
to the E at the top right. How many different ways are there of collecting the nine letters of PINEAPPLE?

ANSWER 201

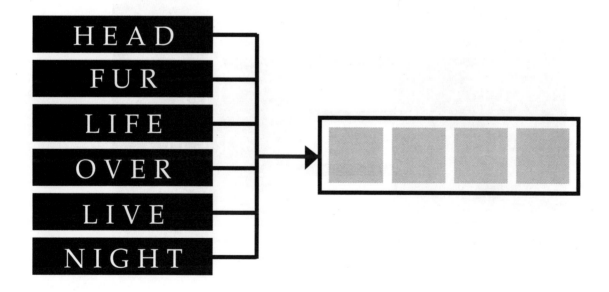

WORD PUZZLE 174

Which English word of four letters can be attached to the back of
the words shown in the diagram to create six other words?

ANSWER 149

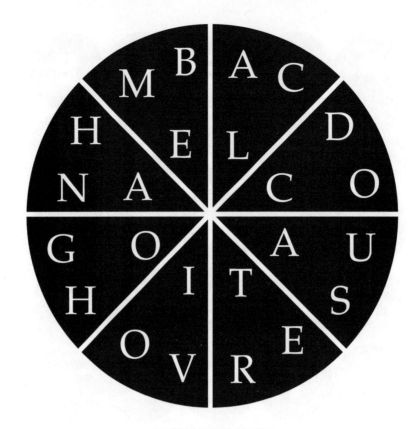

WORD PUZZLE 175

Select one letter from each of the segments.
When the correct letters have been found a word of eight letters
can be read clockwise. What is the word?

ANSWER 190

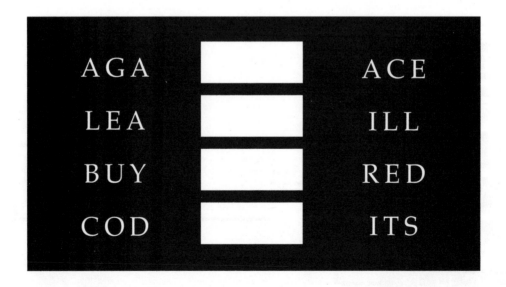

AGA		ACE
LEA		ILL
BUY		RED
COD		ITS

WORD PUZZLE 176

Place two letters in the empty space which, when added to the
words to the left and to the right, form other English words.
When this is completed another word can be read down.
What is the word?

ANSWER 138

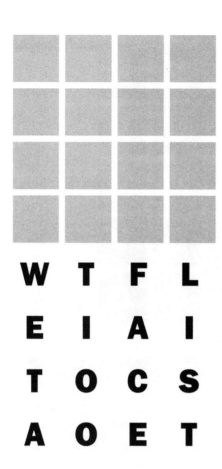

W T F L
E I A I
T O C S
A O E T

WORD PUZZLE 177

Take the letters and arrange them correctly in the column under which they appear. Once this has been done the name of a novel and a movie will emerge. What is it?

ANSWER 180

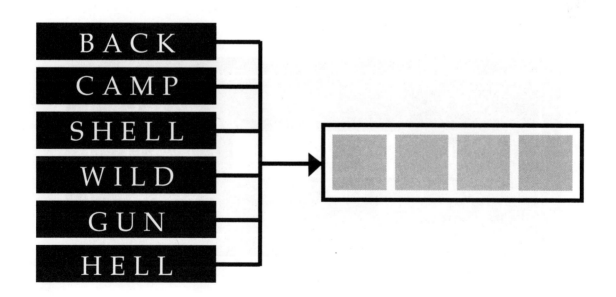

BACK
CAMP
SHELL
WILD
GUN
HELL

WORD PUZZLE 178

Which English word of four letters can be attached to the back of the words shown in the diagram to create six other words?

ANSWER 128

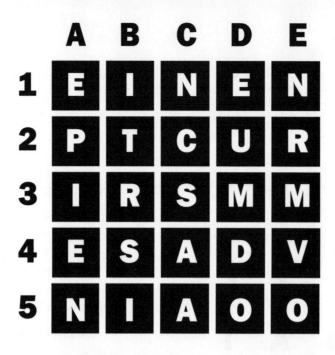

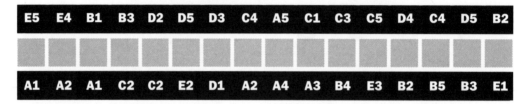

WORD PUZZLE 179

Select one of the two letters from the grid, in accordance with the
reference shown, and place it in the word frame. When the correct
letters have been chosen a sixteen-letter word can be read.
What is the word?

ANSWER 170

WORD PUZZLE 180

Place an English word of THREE letters in the empty space. This
word, when added to the end of the three words to the left and to
the beginning of the three words to the right, will form six other
words. What is the word?

ANSWER 118

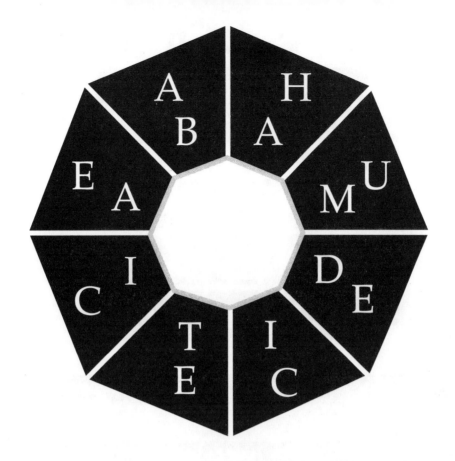

WORD PUZZLE 181

Place one letter in the middle of this diagram. Four five-letter
words can now be rearranged from each straight line of letters.
What is the letter and what are the words?

ANSWER 159

WORD PUZZLE 182

Place an English word of THREE letters in the empty space. This
word, when added to the end of the three words to the left and to
the beginning of the three words to the right, will form six other
words. What is the word?

ANSWER 107

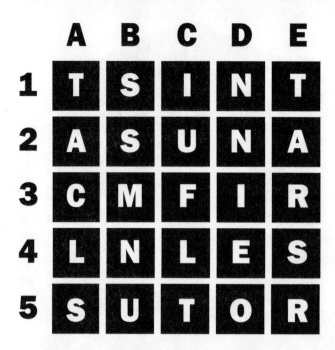

	A	B	C	D	E
1	T	S	I	N	T
2	A	S	U	N	A
3	C	M	F	I	R
4	L	N	L	E	S
5	S	U	T	O	R

D3	B4	B5	A1	A4	C2	D3	D4	D1	A2	A3	A4	D2	B2	D5	E3
C2	B1	A5	E2	E5	C4	B3	E1	C3	E1	E2	A1	C1	D2	C5	E4

WORD PUZZLE 183

Select one of the two letters from the grid, in accordance with the reference shown, and place it in the word frame. When the correct letters have been chosen a sixteen-letter word can be read. What is the word?

ANSWER 200

THE CAVE MAN SAT IN FRONT OF

THE FIRE, HOLDING A

PIECE OF • • • • • ON HIS KNEE, ON

WHICH WAS TO BE FOUND

SOME • • • • • • FOOD.

WORD PUZZLE 184

Two words using the same letters in their construction can be used to replace the dots in this sentence. The sentence will then make sense. Each dot is one letter. What are the words?

ANSWER 148

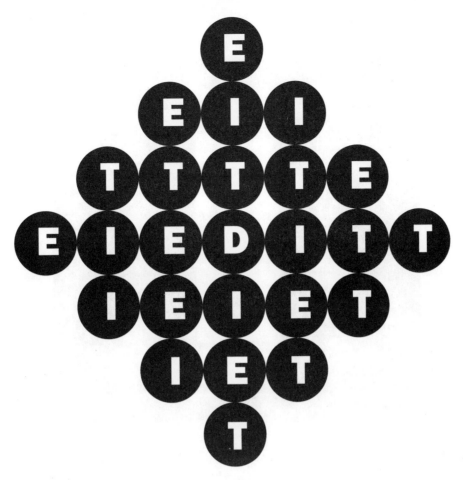

WORD PUZZLE 185

Move from circle to touching circle collecting the letters of DIET.
Always start at the D.
How many different ways are there to do this?

ANSWER 189

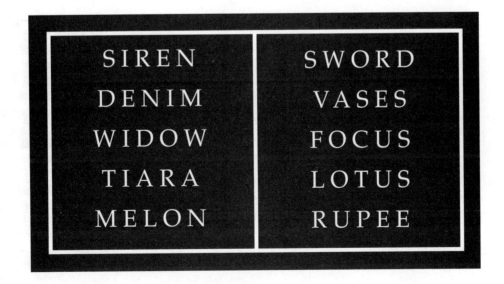

SIREN	SWORD
DENIM	VASES
WIDOW	FOCUS
TIARA	LOTUS
MELON	RUPEE

WORD PUZZLE 186

Five of the words in the diagram are associated for some
reason. Find the words and then work out whether VISOR belongs
to the group.

ANSWER 137

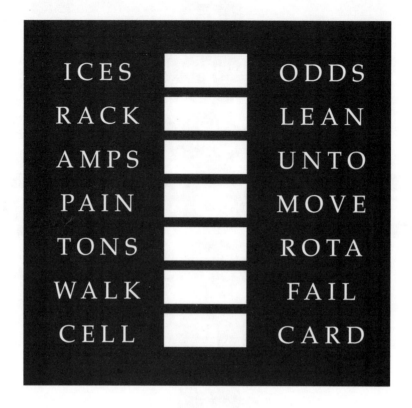

WORD PUZZLE 187

Change the first letter of each word to the left and the right. Two other English words must be formed. Place the letter used in the empty section. When this has been completed for all the words another English word can be read down. What is the word?

ANSWER 179

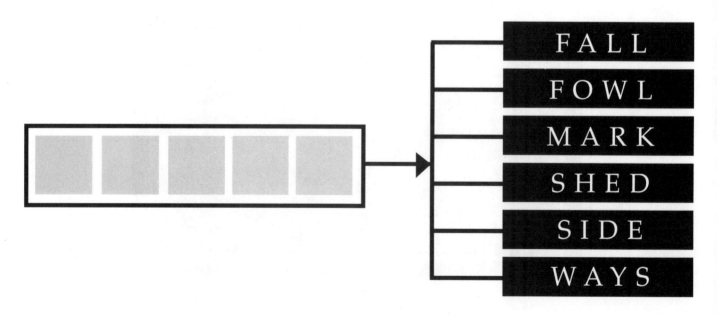

WORD PUZZLE 188

Which English word of five letters can be attached to the front of the words shown in the diagram to create six other words?

ANSWER 127

GRAPE

PEACH

WORD PUZZLE 189

Complete the word ladder by changing one letter of each word
per step. The newly created word must be found in the dictionary.
What are the words to turn GRAPE to PEACH?

ANSWER 169

D	N	O	T	S	K
E	F	W	H	E	A
R	R	O	H	E	M
G	R	E	S	C	E
T	A	B	A	E	N

WORD PUZZLE 190

A proverb has been written in this diagram. Find the start letter
and move from square to touching square until you have found it.
What is it?

ANSWER 117

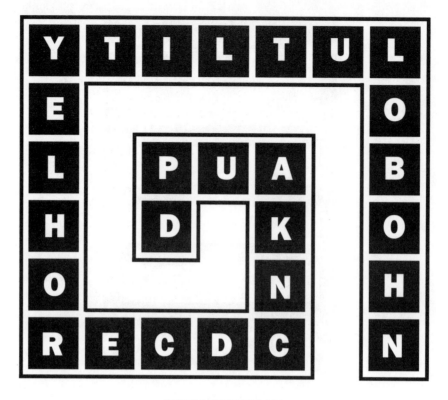

WORD PUZZLE 191

The names of three flowers are to be found in the diagram.
The letters of the names are in the order they normally appear.
What are the flowers?

ANSWER 158

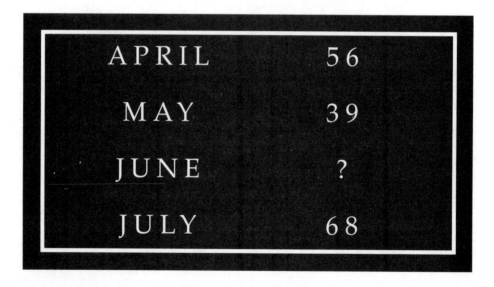

APRIL	56
MAY	39
JUNE	?
JULY	68

WORD PUZZLE 192

The diagram shows the sunshine hours in England for four
months . The numbers bear a relationship to the letters in the
words. What should replace the question mark?

ANSWER 106

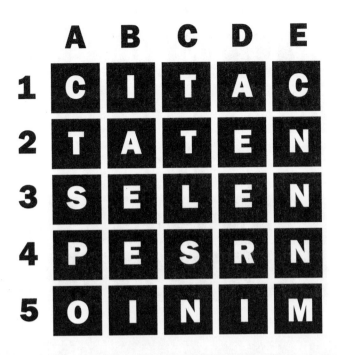

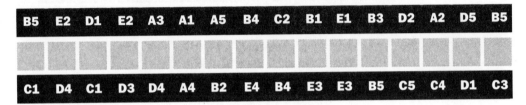

WORD PUZZLE 193

Select one of the two letters from the grid, in accordance with the reference shown, and place it in the word frame. When the correct letters have been chosen a sixteen-letter word can be read.
What is the word?

ANSWER 199

THE WEIGHT LIFTER, ALTHOUGH

VERY • • • • • • , FAILED IN HIS

ATTEMPT BECAUSE OF HIS

• • • • • • • APPROACH.

WORD PUZZLE 194

Two words using the same letters in their construction can be used to replace the dots in this sentence. The sentence will then make sense. Each dot is one letter. What are the words?

ANSWER 147

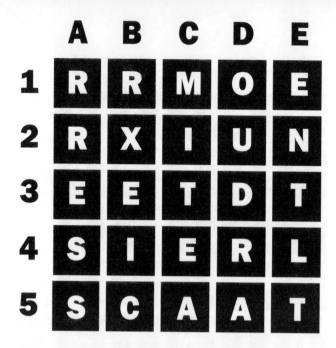

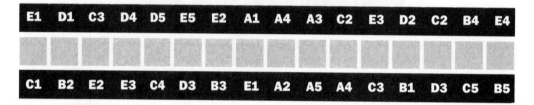

WORD PUZZLE 195

Select one of the two letters from the grid, in accordance with the reference shown, and place it in the word frame. When the correct letters have been chosen a sixteen-letter word can be read. What is the word?

ANSWER 188

WORD PUZZLE 196

Make a circle out of these shapes.
When the correct circle has been found a word can be read clockwise. What is the word?

ANSWER 136

R M S E
A O H O
F T E N
T H E E

WORD PUZZLE 197

Take the letters and arrange
them correctly in the column
under which they appear.
Once this has been done the name
of a movie will emerge.
What is it?

ANSWER 178

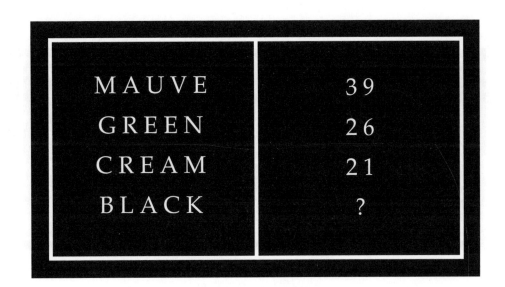

MAUVE	39
GREEN	26
CREAM	21
BLACK	?

WORD PUZZLE 198

On this list of four colours the numbers bear a relationship to the
letters in the words. What should replace the question mark?

ANSWER 126

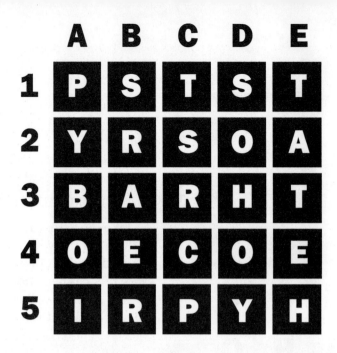

	A	B	C	D	E
1	P	S	T	S	T
2	Y	R	S	O	A
3	B	A	R	H	T
4	O	E	C	O	E
5	I	R	P	Y	H

| C5 | E4 | D1 | E1 | D3 | D2 | D4 | E5 | B5 | B2 | B3 | A1 | B4 | C2 | C4 | D3 |

| C1 | B1 | A2 | C4 | E2 | E3 | E1 | A4 | E4 | C3 | D5 | A3 | A5 | B3 | C1 | D1 |

WORD PUZZLE 199

Select one of the two letters from the grid, in accordance with the
reference shown, and place it in the word frame. When the correct
letters have been chosen a sixteen-letter word can be read.
What is the word?

ANSWER 168

THE PYTHON WOUND

•••••• AROUND THE VICTIM

AS IT ATTEMPTED TO ••••••

IT TO DEATH.

WORD PUZZLE 200

Two words using the same letters in their construction can be used
to replace the dots in this sentence. The sentence will then make
sense. Each dot is one letter. What are the words?

ANSWER 116

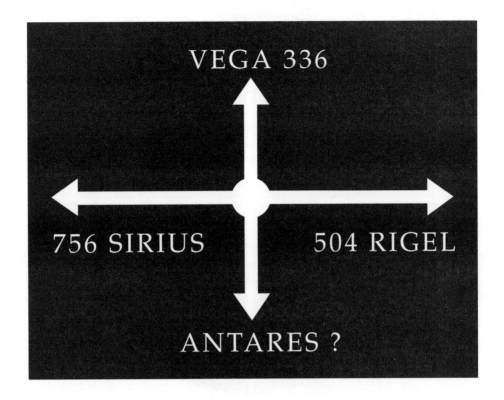

WORD PUZZLE 201

The diagram shows the light years to various stars. The numbers
bear a relationship to the letters in the words. What should replace
the question mark?

ANSWER 157

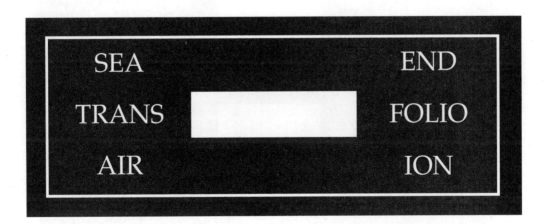

WORD PUZZLE 202

Place an English word of FOUR letters in the empty space. This
word, when added to the end of the three words to the left and to
the beginning of the three words to the right, will form six other
words. What is the word?

ANSWER 105

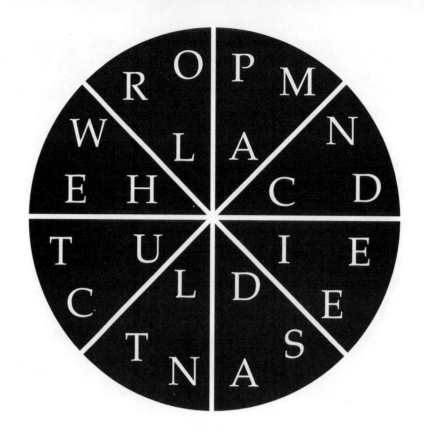

WORD PUZZLE 203

Select one letter from each of the segments.
When the correct letters have been found a word of eight letters
can be read clockwise. What is the word?

ANSWER 198

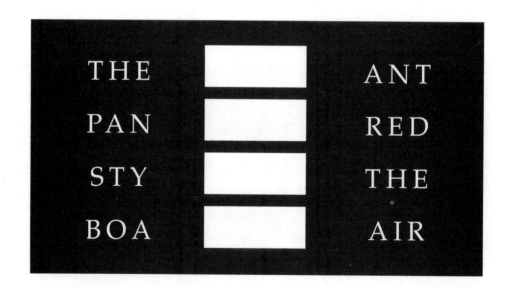

WORD PUZZLE 204

Place two letters in the empty space which, when added to the
words to the left and to the right, form other English words.
When this is completed another word can be read down.
What is the word?

ANSWER 146

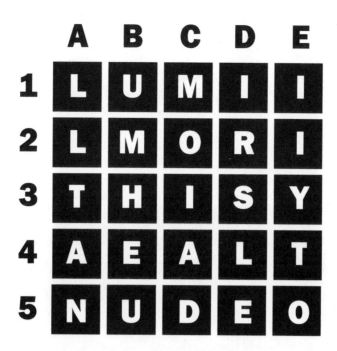

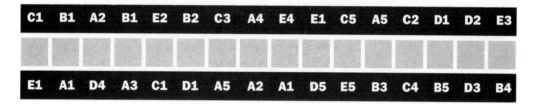

WORD PUZZLE 205

Select one of the two letters from the grid, in accordance with the
reference shown, and place it in the word frame. When the correct
letters have been chosen a sixteen-letter word can be read.
What is the word?

ANSWER 187

IN THE FOREST

FIRE THE UNDERGROWTH

• • • • • • • IN THE FLAMES

AS THE TREE • • • • • • • .

WORD PUZZLE 206

Two words using the same letters in their construction can be used
to replace the dots in this sentence. The sentence will then make
sense. Each dot is one letter. What are the words?

ANSWER 135

Answers

1. Ohm, Stoop, Respond, and Chop.

2. Word, Oboe, Rode, and Deep.

3. Mow, Jewel, Blanket, and Down.

4. Back, Aeon, Cove, and Knew.

5. Ivy, Geese, Embrace, and Over.

6. Yard, Afar, Race, and Drew.

7. Fir, First, Firearm, and Fire.

8. Stop, Tame, Omen, and Pent.

9. Lid, Valid, Quality, and Will.

10. Tide, Idea, Deer, and Ears.

11. Fire.

12. Rulers have no authority from God to do mischief. Jonathan Mayhew.

13. Bird.

14. The first casualty when war comes is truth. Hiram Johnson.

15. Well.

16. All animals are equal but some animals are more equal than others. George Orwell.

17. Like.

18. If you can't stand the heat keep out of the kitchen. President Harry Truman.

19. Den.

20. When you have to kill a man it costs nothing to be polite. Winston Churchill.

21. Rugged and Grudge.

22. Low.

23. Misunderstanding.

24. Buck.

25. 192. Each vowel is worth 6 and each consonant 8. The vowels are added together, as are the consonants. The totals are then multiplied.

26. Foot.

27. Brides and Debris.

28. Hand.

29. 21 ways.

30. Moon.

31. Tolerate.

32. Flute does not belong to the group. The five associated words are Decoy, Steam, Tulip, Abbey, and Hippo. The first two letters of each word are in alphabetical order.

33. Delegate.

34. 12 ways.

35. Imposter.

36. 8 ways.

37. Operator.

38. 9 ways.

39. Reunites.

40. Shell does not belong to the group. The linked words are Beast, Decor, Heron, Human, Pilaf, and Round. The first and last letter position in the alphabet totals 22.

41. Daffodil.

42. Nest.

43. Baseball.

44. Cast.

45. Woodbine.

46. Band.

47. Taxpayer.

48. Step.

49. Aardvark.

50. House.

51. Kindness.

52. B. To give Elbow, Orbit, Habit, and Noble.

53. Satinwood, Jacaranda, and Greengage.

54. A. To give Koala, Peace, Shade, and Whale.

55. Cannelloni, Macaroni, and Spaghetti.

56. J. To give Enjoy, Major, Rajah, and Dojos.

57. Champagne, Chocolate, and Orangeade.

58. H. To give Abhor, Ethic, Ochre (or Chore), and Usher.

59. Harmonium, Accordion, Piano, and Tuba.

60. P. To give Capon, Hippo, Imply, and Paper.

61. Argentina, Australia, and Indonesia.

62. G. To give Angel, Anger (or Range), Cigar, and Logic.

63. 27. Each vowel is worth 2 and each consonant 3. The totals of the vowels and consonants are added.

64. Loon, Loop, Poop, Pomp, Pump.

65. 20. Each vowel is worth 4 and each consonant 2. The totals of the vowels and consonants are added.

66. Bony, Bone, Cone, Cane, Care.

67. Summer Vacations.

68. Raver, Raves, Paves, Pares, Bares, Barks.

69. 57. Each letter is given its positional value in the alphabet and these are added together.

70. Shop, Shoe, Sloe, Floe, Flee, Free.

71. 108. Each vowel in the name is worth 10 and each consonant is worth 22. These are all added together to give the distance.

72. Sleds, Slews, Slows, Glows, Grows, Gross.

73. Benjamin Franklin.

74. Gesture.

75. Dances with Wolves.

76. Rainbow.

77. The Spy Who Loved Me.

78. Emerald.

79. Oscar Hammerstein.

80. Magenta.

81. Mary, Queen of Scots.

82. Crimson.

83. Nineteen.

84. 17 ways.

85. Journals.

86. Style belongs to the group. The linked words are Abyss, Buyer, Coypu, Idyll, and Mayor. All of these words have Y as the third letter.

87. Historic.

88. Syrup does not belong to the group. The linked words are Cedar, Hedge, Medal, Sedan, and Wedge. All the words contain ED.

89. February.

90. Plant belongs to the group. The linked words are Burnt, Count, Event, Flint, and Giant. All the words end in NT.

91. Caffeine.

92. 5 ways

93. Unconstitutional.

94. 26 ways.

95. Disqualification.

96. 9 ways.

97. Characterization.

98. 22 ways.

99. Air-conditioning.

100. 14 ways.

101. Thanksgiving day.

102. 25 ways.

103. Acknowledgements.

104. Tango, Alien, Nines, Geese, and

105. Port.

106. 50. The alphabetical values of the letters are added together.

107. Ten.

108. Sat, Bacon, Anchors, and Each.

109. Yeast, Eager, Agave, Seven, and Trend.

110. Cot, Attic, Cushion, and Both.

111. Facet, Above, Coven, Event, and Tents.

112. Ripens and Sniper.

113. Smile, Mania, Inset, Liege, and Eater.

114. Arm, Enter, Mansion, and Arts.

115. Cheer does belong to the group. The associated words are Jetty, Comma, Annoy, Caddy, and Steel. Each have double letters.

116. Itself and Stifle.

117. Absence makes the heart grow fonder.

118. Eye.

119. Every man meets his Waterloo at last. Wendell Phillips.

120. Umpire and Impure.

121. Die my dear doctor thats the last thing I shall do. Lord Palmerston.

122. Her.

123. One more such victory and we are lost. Pyrrhus.

124. End.

125. 6 ways.

126. 14. The alphabetical values of the first, third and fifth letters are added together.

127. Water.

128. Fire.

129. Flat.

130. Dance, Acorn, Nomad, Crave, and Ended.

131. Met, Amaze, Chamber, and Team.

132. Had, Blink, Academy, and Raid.

133. Ram.

134. Fantasy.

135. Writhes and Withers.

136. Macaroni.

137. Visor belongs to the group. The associated words are Vases, Denim, Widow, Focus, and Lotus. In each word the vowels appear in alphabetical order.

138. Pestered.

139. Globe does not belong to the group. The associated words are Hymns, Light, Ankle, Films, Index, and Pasta. Each word contains two letters next to each other which appear consecutively in the alphabet.

140. Deadline.

141. Widow belongs to the group. The associated words are Dread, Kiosk, Loyal, Arena, and Comic. Each word begins and ends with the same letter.

142. Teaspoon.

143. Cafes belongs to the group. The associated words are Babes, Games, Cakes, Paper, and Tales. Each have A and E as their second and fourth letter.

144. Gathered.

145. Comment is free but facts are sacred. C.P. Scott.

146. Medalist.

147. Muscly and Clumsy.

148. Slate and Stale.

149. Long.

150. Jealousy.

151. Red.

152. Suitcase.

153. Boy.

154. Gardener.

155. Man.

156. Sun.

157. 1008. Each consonant is worth 7 and each vowel 12. The consonant total is multiplied by the vowel total.

158. Hollyhock, Buttercup, and Dandelion.

159. S. To give Basic, Eased, Haste (or Heats), and Music.

160. Butterfly, Centipede, and Cockroach.

161. E. To give Agent, Bleak, Enemy, and Query.

162. Decorator, Policeman, and Architect.

163. V. To give Civic, Devil (or Lived), Haven, and Lever.

164. Coriander, Asparagus, and Artichoke.

165. K. To give Joked, Maker, Taken, and Yokel.

166. Wolverine , Armadillo, and Porcupine.

167. 16 ways.

168. Psychotherapists.

169. Grace, Glace, Place, Peace.

170. Overcompensation.

171. Sort, Soot, Shot, Shop.

172. Responsibilities.

173. Prop, Poop, Pool, Poll, Pall.

174. 114. A is given the value 6, B is given 7 and so forth. The letter values in each word are added together.

175. Stare, Stars, Stays, Slays.

176. 57. The first and last [ALL] letters are given the value of their position in the alphabet. These are then added together.

177. 5 ways.

178. The Name of the Rose.

179. Ability.

180. A Tale of Two Cities.

181. Badgers.

182. Star Trek the Movie.

183. Calypso.

184. George Washington.

185. Delight.

186. Winston Churchill.

187. Multimillionaire.

188. Extraterrestrial.

189. 11 ways.

190. Macaroon

191. 18 ways.

192. Ultimate.

193. 16 ways.

194. Horsefly.

195. 21 ways.

196. Puzzlers.

197. Glaze, Glare, Glary.

198. Radiance.

199. Intercontinental.

200. Instrumentalists.

201. 10 ways.

202. Enthusiastically.

203. Crated and Carted.

204. Conservationists.

205. 8 ways.

206. Subconsciousness.